The Brownie Scouts at Windmill Farm

"Mrs. Gabriel has her flashlight turned on now."
Brownie Scouts at Windmill Farm   See Page 178

The
BROWNIE SCOUTS
at Windmill Farm

by

Mildred A. Wirt

ILLUSTRATED

CUPPLES AND LEON COMPANY
Publishers New York

Copyright, 1953, by
CUPPLES AND LEON COMPANY

ALL RIGHTS RESERVED

The Brownie Scouts at Windmill Farm

Printed in the United States of America

CONTENTS

Chapter		Page
1.	The Dog Cart	1
2.	Hanny to the Rescue	14
3.	Mr. Piff's Plan	23
4.	The Little Locked House	31
5.	Hanny's Secret	41
6.	Wooden Shoes	52
7.	A Runaway 'Boat'	63
8.	The Treasure House	71
9.	High Wind	80
10.	In the Hayloft	89
11.	The Man in Gray	102
12.	A Flower Show	116
13.	A Bag of Tulips	127
14.	Mr. Piff's Troubles	136
15.	The Brownie Garden	148
16.	Mrs. Gabriel's Accusation	156
17.	A Library Window	166
18.	Magic Ways	176
19.	An Announcement	189
20.	Surprise!	200

Chapter 1

THE DOG CART

FIVE pair of eyes focused with rapt attention upon Miss Paula Mohr, the librarian.

Five little girls in pin-checked Brownie Scout uniforms had been listening attentively to a tale about the children of Holland.

Now, in the story room of the Rosedale Public Library, they awaited an important announcement.

"Girls," began Miss Mohr. She was young and pretty, and her voice had soft edges. "How would the Brownies like to help this spring with Rosedale's annual tulip show?"

"Oh, fine and dandy!" cried Vevi McGuire.

The dark-eyed little girl shouted approval, even without asking what the Brownies would be expected to do. But then, she knew anything planned by Miss Mohr or Miss Jean Gordon, the Brownie troop leader, would be fun.

"Will we sell things?" inquired Connie Williams.

Connie was the quiet, thoughtful member of the

1

The Brownie Scouts at Windmill Farm

group. Sometimes the other Brownies, Rosemary Fritche, Sunny Davidson and Jane Tuttle, teased her by calling her "the thinker."

"Oh, no," replied Miss Mohr. "I am not sure of the plans, but we would assist Mrs. Langley."

The Brownie Scouts all knew that Mrs. Langley was president of the Rosedale Garden Club. She lived with her servants on a large estate of many acres at the edge of town.

Each spring when bulbs bloomed, her gardens were the most beautiful in Rosedale.

"May we help Mrs. Langley?" asked Jane Tuttle, with a toss of her long pigtails. She directed the question at Miss Gordon.

"Why, yes," the troop leader promptly agreed. "I think the project would be a most worthwhile one."

"When will Rosedale have its flower show?" inquired Sunny Davidson.

Miss Mohr explained that the exact date had not yet been set. It would depend, she said, upon the weather, and when the tulips reached the climax of bloom.

"This year Mrs. Langley hopes to interest all garden growers and possibly the commercial raisers," she added. "We want our show to be the best ever!"

The Dog Cart

"Speaking of commercial growers, reminds me of something!" spoke up Miss Gordon. "Do you girls know Peter Van Der Lann?"

The Brownies had never heard the name. Miss Mohr however, knew it well.

"Peter Van Der Lann is the young Dutchman who started a tulip nursery here last fall," she declared. "His little niece, Hanny, often comes to the library to read."

"A charming little girl," added Miss Gordon warmly. "Just the right age to be a Brownie too— eight, I believe."

The Brownies now were very quiet, thinking about Hanny. Then Connie spoke.

"I saw her once, I think. She was buying a lollypop at the drugstore. She had long shining yellow braids and very blue eyes. But she wore big wooden shoes!"

"*Klompen*," supplied Miss Mohr, using the Dutch name. "Hanny only wore them when she first came to Rosedale months ago. She wears regular American shoes now. She has improved her English a great deal too."

"Would she want to be a Brownie Scout?" Jane Tuttle asked, doubt in her voice.

"I'm certain she would," replied Miss Gordon. "Holland has a Brownie organization too, you know. There, Brownies are called *Kabouters* which means Little Elves."

The girls plied Miss Gordon with eager questions about Hanny and the country from which she had come.

In the midst of the conversation, someone tapped lightly on the door of the story room. Another librarian entered to speak to Miss Mohr.

"I am so sorry to interrupt," she apologized. "A caller is here by the name of Ashley Piff. He insists upon seeing both Miss Mohr and Miss Gordon. He says it is about the garden show."

Neither Miss Gordon nor the librarian ever had heard of anyone named Mr. Piff.

"I'll see him," Miss Mohr decided. "The Brownie meeting was just ending anyway."

She reminded the girls not to forget the regular story hour the following week. Then with Miss Gordon she went out into the main reading room to talk to the stranger.

The Brownies donned their beanies and jackets. Gathering up their school books, they too sauntered outside.

The Dog Cart

Mr. Piff was a short, stubby man with a black derby hat. He spoke too loudly for the library. His words carried clearly to every part of the quiet room.

"Now this is my proposition," the Brownies heard him say. "I am a professional promoter of flower shows. If you ring me in on the deal, I'll put on a celebration that will be the talk of the town for years! We'll lift your little show out of the amateur class, and make it a hum-dinger. What d'you say?"

"You really must see Mrs. Langley," replied Miss Mohr. "She is in charge. Personally though, I'm not in favor of turning our lovely garden show into a cheap commercial festival."

"Nor am I," added Miss Gordon firmly.

"You don't get the idea," protested Mr. Piff. "It would be a commercial project—true. There would be money in it for everyone. Rosedale and all the merchants would profit. The Brownies—"

"Our organization cannot take part in such an enterprise," Miss Gordon said emphatically. "We have promised to help Mrs. Langley with the annual garden show. That however, is an entirely different matter."

Mr. Piff realized that he could not change the teacher's mind.

"Okay, if that's your decision," he said. "You'll regret it though. Now can you direct me to the nursery of Peter Van Der Lann?"

Miss Mohr showed Mr. Piff on a map how to reach the nearby farm.

"I'll never find the place by myself," he said. "How about driving out there with me?"

Miss Mohr started to refuse, but before she could do so, Mr. Piff went on:

"Isn't it nearly closing time here at the library?"

"In ten minutes. But—"

"It shouldn't take long to drive out to the nursery," Mr. Piff said briskly. "My car is at the door. Now it would be a great favor to a stranger who doesn't know the community. I'll take anyone who wants to go, and bring you back too."

Miss Mohr really did not care to make the trip. But Mr. Piff was very persuasive. He pointed out that it was a lovely afternoon for a drive in the country. Finally, he convinced both young women that they should accompany him.

"May we go too?" demanded Vevi. She always liked to ride in a car.

Her request did not appear to please Mr. Piff. He managed to smile though, and said he would take

The Dog Cart

as many Brownies as the sedan would accommodate.

"I have to go home right away," spoke up Jane.

"So do I," said Sunny.

Rosemary also turned down the invitation. Vevi and Connie were the only two Brownies to go. They sat in the back seat of the big brown sedan, while Miss Mohr and Miss Gordon rode up front with Mr. Piff.

As the car sped along the open country road, the promotor talked at great length. He kept telling the two young women about his elaborate plans for the flower festival.

"I want to interest every tulip grower in the community," he said grandly. "This will be the biggest affair Rosedale has ever had!"

Connie and Vevi fairly tingled with excitement to hear Mr. Piff describe everything he intended to do.

The Brownie leader and Miss Mohr were less impressed. In fact, both women seemed rather relieved when finally the car came within view of the Van Der Lann nursery.

"Oh, see the cute Dutch windmill!" cried Vevi as the car rolled over a hilltop.

The tower-like wooden building stood nearly fifty feet high on a slight rise of land. Because it had been painted red, blue and green, the unique structure could be seen from a long distance. Four large wind flaps turned lazily in the breeze.

"Oh, how lovely!" exclaimed Miss Gordon, who never before had seen the mill. "Why, it looks like a charming bit of Old Holland!"

Two stone gate piers marked the entrance to the farm. The house was gabled, with a red tile roof which sloped forward to cover a wide veranda. Beyond stood the big barn and a small milk house. Everywhere there were acres and acres of tulips. Only a few of the flowers as yet were in bloom.

"This place will be a sea of color in a week or so!" exclaimed Miss Mohr. "I'd love to see it then."

"We'll have the show when the flowers are at their best," said Mr. Piff. He leaped out of the car to open the gate.

Returning, he drove through and pulled up in front of the house. Vevi and Connie jumped out, eager to explore. The farm was a delightful place, neat as a pin. Even the trees had been whitewashed.

As the two little girls stood watching the huge revolving arms of the windmill, a nice looking young man came out of the house. His shirt was

The Dog Cart

open at the neck and he was deeply tanned from having lived much of the time outdoors.

"Good afternoon," he said, walking over to the car. "May I help you?"

Vevi and Connie noticed that instead of saying Good, the word sounded a little like "goot." They guessed at once that he was Mr. Van Der Lann, the owner of the nursery.

Mr. Piff introduced himself and at once began to tell of his plans for the flower show.

Not caring to listen, Vevi and Connie wandered off down the cinder path.

"Oh, see!" cried Vevi pointing ahead. "A little canal! The windmill must pump water from it to irrigate the tulip beds."

The path which led to the canal went directly past the big windmill. Its great arms were covered with gray sailcloth which moved lazily in the light breeze. The big flaps swept low to the ground each time they revolved.

"The windmill has a little house!" Vevi declared. "That must be where the machinery is kept."

"I've never been inside a real mill," Connie remarked wistfully.

The Brownie Scouts at Windmill Farm

"Neither have I. I'd like to go in. Shall we?"

Connie held back. "I don't think it would be polite, Vevi. We're only half-way guests here on the farm. Mr. Van Der Lann didn't even invite us. We just came with Mr. Piff."

For awhile the children watched the mill, and then went on down to the canal. A little bridge of planks stretched across to the opposite side.

Both shores were lined with tulips, heavy with bud. All of the beds had been laid out in attractive patterns.

"My, it will be pretty here when the flowers bloom," Vevi sighed. "No wonder Mr. Piff wants Mr. Van Der Lann to help with the flower show! This place would be a big attraction."

Vevi noticed a small flat-bottomed boat tied up near the bridge. Its name, "GOLDEN TULIP," had been painted in bright yellow letters on the craft.

"What an odd name for a boat!" she exclaimed. "Let's take a ride."

"We can't," Connie replied firmly. "Anyway, the canal might be deep."

"Why, it's shallow as anything," Vevi corrected her. "I can see the bottom."

"We shouldn't do it anyway. Miss Gordon wouldn't like it."

The Dog Cart

Connie knew that she must be firm, for Vevi had a way of getting into trouble. Once she had hooked her sled onto an automobile, and had been carried far out into the country. On another occasion the little girl had climbed into a box car to be taken off with a circus!

"I wonder where the canal leads?" Vevi speculated, giving up the idea of a boat ride.

The children could see that the canal wound along rich farm land toward another nursery property. However, the adjoining farm did not look as well laid out or as nicely kept as Mr. Van der Lann's place.

After tossing a stick into the canal, the girls decided it must be time to return to the house.

They were recrossing the bridge when Vevi suddenly halted.

Connie, directly behind, bumped into her.

"What's the idea, Vevi McGuire?" she demanded. "You nearly made me fall into the water!"

Vevi spoke in an excited, hushed voice. "Connie, just see what is coming!"

She moved aside so that her little friend's view would not be blocked. The barn doors had swung open, and now, clattering toward them, was a cart hauled by a huge dog.

"Well, did you ever!" exclaimed Connie, laughing in delight.

The little cart had two wheels. It was painted bright blue and held empty milk cans.

Hurrying on across the bridge, the two girls ran toward the dog. Even though he had no driver, he seemed to know exactly where he was supposed to go. At least he trotted toward the milk house farther down the canal.

"Hello, doggie," Vevi called in a soft voice. "What's your name?"

To her astonishment, the dog stopped and looked at her. He was a very large dog, but with a sad, kind face.

"Why, he's friendly as anything!" Connie exclaimed.

"Mr. Van Der Lann must own him," Vevi said. Carefully, she petted the dog's head. "Oh, don't you just love this place? I'd like to live here."

"So you could go boating on the canal and ride in the dog cart!" teased Connie.

"Well, it would be fun."

Vevi gazed speculatively at the cart. She could see that there was room to slide in behind the empty milk cans.

The Dog Cart

Before Connie could stop her, she climbed in and picked up the reins.

"Oh, Vevi!" Connie protested. "You're too heavy for that poor dog to haul."

"I'm light as a feather," Vevi insisted. "Get up, doggie!"

She made a loud clucking noise to make him go.

The dog started off so fast that Vevi nearly was tossed backwards out of the cart.

"Hey, come back!" Connie shouted. She saw that the dog had headed straight for the canal.

Vevi squealed in fear. The cart was rattling down the slope, faster and faster. One of the empty milk cans toppled over, making a frightful clatter.

The sound startled the dog. He bounded on, even faster.

"Whoa!" Vevi shouted, and tried to pull back on the reins. But she was too frightened. Dropping them entirely, she clung desperately to the side of the jolting cart.

"H-E-L-P," she called. "Save me, Connie! Stop him quick before he dumps me into the canal!"

Chapter 2

HANNY TO THE RESCUE

CONNIE tried to dart ahead of the cart. She could not move quickly enough to stop the runaway dog.

On the cart clattered, directly toward the canal. Off rolled one of the milk cans and Vevi nearly went with it. Never in her life had she been more jolted or frightened!

When it seemed to her that she certainly would be dumped into the canal, an amazing thing happened.

Out of the barn darted a little girl in shining yellow braids, blue skirt and white apron.

"Bruno!" she yelled. Then she uttered a command in Dutch. Vevi could not understand it, but the dog did. At any rate, he stopped so suddenly that she nearly was tossed out of the cart again.

Connie grasped the dog's harness. Vevi slid out of the cart as fast as she could.

"You bad dog, you!" she said crossly.

Hanny to the Rescue

The little girl in the blue dress came running up. Her blue eyes were dancing with merriment.

"Oh, Bruno isn't a bad dog," she defended him. "He is a very good dog. He carries our milk and does much hard work here on the farm."

"Well, he nearly dumped me into the canal," Vevi said, straightening the crumpled skirt of her Brownie uniform.

"That was because you did not treat him right. If you would like a ride in the cart, I will make him haul you very nicely."

"No thanks," Vevi turned down the invitation. "I'd rather ride in a car—or a boat."

"You must be Hanny," said Connie, smiling in a friendly way.

"How did you know my name?" the other asked in surprise.

"Miss Mohr, the librarian told us."

"Oh, I know her!" Hanny cried, and her plump face lighted up. "She is very nice."

"So is Miss Gordon, our Brownie Scout leader," declared Vevi loyally. "They are here now, with Mr. Piff, talking to Mr. Van Der Lann."

"With Peter? He is my uncle."

Hanny straightened the milk cans and then made Bruno haul them to the cheese house. The dog behaved very well when she walked beside him. Not once did he try to run away.

Vevi and Connie walked along with the little Dutch girl.

"Why do you call your boat the "Golden Tulip?" Vevi inquired.

"Oh, that is a secret," replied Hanny.

"A secret?" Vevi was annoyed by the answer. She could not guess why anyone would want to make a mystery of such a simple matter.

"Someday everyone in Rosedale will know," Hanny went on merrily. "Then perhaps my uncle will be very rich and buy me a silk gown!"

"How you talk!" Vevi exclaimed. Never before had she met anyone like Hanny.

Connie mentioned the boat again, asking the little Dutch girl if she ever went for rides on the canal.

"Oh, yes, but not as often as I once did," Hanny said, her face clouding. "That is because of Freda and Joseph."

"Who are they?" Vevi inquired.

"Freda and Joseph Mattox," Hanny replied. "They

have the farm just below ours. They are not very nice and always make trouble. They will not let me tie up the boat anywhere on their land."

"You have a much prettier farm than theirs," said Connie. "The windmill is lovely."

"Do you think so?" Hanny beamed with pleasure. "My uncle has spent much money fixing up the farm so it will remind him of our beautiful homeland. The Mattoxes, though, say he is wasteful of money. It is not true!"

The little girl unloaded the empty milk cans. Then she unhitched Bruno and let him run free.

"Would you like to see our cheese house?" she invited Connie and Vevi.

"Yes, indeed!" they exclaimed together. Both were eager to see every inch of the fascinating farm.

Hanny pushed open the door and stood back so the visitors could enter ahead of her. The room was sweet-smelling and spotlessly clean.

Along the walls were deep shelves laden with yellow, perfectly rounded cheeses. Fresh milk stood on tables in blue and orange-colored pans.

"Each morning I skim the cream and churn it into butter," explained Hanny.

"You know how to churn?" Connie asked, deeply impressed.

The Brownie Scouts at Windmill Farm

"Oh, yes, I can make cheese too. We use the skimmed milk for that. I add rennet which makes the solids separate from the liquid. The curds or solid part goes into a bag to be pressed out. After it is salted, it is set away to ripen. That takes several months."

"How do you make the cheese into such nice round balls?" Connie inquired, peering at the many even rows on the shelves.

Hanny explained that wooden molds were used. "But it is hard work, making cheese," she added with a sigh.

"I should think so," agreed Vevi. "I would rather run the windmill or make the dog carry the cans of milk."

By this time the Brownies were beginning to feel very well acquainted with Hanny. They no longer noticed that she spoke with a slight accent or that sometimes she slipped in a "Ja" for the word "yes." Connie told the little Dutch girl about the Rosedale Brownie Scout organization and asked if she would like to join the group.

"What do Brownies do?" asked Hanny.

"Loads of things," explained Connie. "We make things and learn about nature. To be a Brownie you

Hanny to the Rescue

can't be older than nine years. You're supposed to be in second, third or fourth grade at school."

"I am all mixed up at school," Hanny said. "In arithmetic I am fourth grade, but in English I am only second grade. I do not know so many of your words."

"That doesn't matter," Vevi declared. "Attending meetings is what counts. You have to learn the Brownie Promise too."

"What is that?"

Vevi recited it for her. "*I promise to do my best to love God and my country, to help other people every day, especially those at home.*"

"I could promise all that," Hanny said soberly. "I love America very, very much. I want to help people too, especially my uncle, Peter. If it had not been for him, I never could have left The Netherlands."

The little Dutch girl then went on to tell Vevi and Connie that until recently she had lived in a little village near the city of Amsterdam. Both of her parents were dead.

"I have no one in all the world except Peter," she said. "He is very good to me."

Vevi felt so sorry for Hanny that she unpinned

her Brownie Scout pin and fastened it to the other's blouse.

"Now you can pretend you're a Brownie," she declared. "When you get a pin of your own, you can return mine."

"After you have been a Brownie for a year, you may wear a flower pendant with it," Connie explained. "Both Vevi and I have pendants."

Indeed, the two girls were charter members of the Rosedale Troop. With Rosemary, Sunny and Jane they had made a wonderful trip to the seashore. On another occasion they had gone with Miss Gordon to Snow Valley. One of their most exciting adventures has been told in the book called "The Brownie Scouts in the Cherry Festival."

Now Connie and Vevi never missed a Brownie meeting if they could help it. In Rosedale they lived next door to each other, and attended the same school. They enjoyed doing the same things too.

"Tell me more about the Brownie Scouts," Hanny said, fingering the pin Vevi had given her.

"First you have to be invested," Connie declared.

The word troubled Hanny. "But I do not have very much money to invest," she said. "My uncle

Hanny to the Rescue

cannot afford to give me much, for his nursery does not yet pay well."

"Oh, that isn't what investment means!" laughed Vevi. "It means joining the organization—being initiated."

"It's a ceremony and it is called in-ves-ti-ture," Connie said, spelling out the word. "You learn the Promise, the Salute, and the Handshake and attend enough meetings to know all the girls. Then you're ready to be a Brownie."

"I see," nodded Hanny. "I am so very stupid."

"No such thing," cried Vevi, seizing her hand. "It always takes a while to catch on. But being a Brownie is fun. We have hikes and do lots of things out of doors. We learn to keep house, too. That part I don't like so well."

"That would be easy for me," laughed Hanny. "I can sweep, iron, and cook! Peter says I am worth two girls in the house!"

The children talked a while about the Brownies and then left the cheese house. Hanny said she would show Connie and Vevi the barn and the mill.

"And what's in that little house over there?" Vevi asked curiously.

The Brownie Scouts at Windmill Farm

The shack she had noticed stood between the mill and the barn. It had no windows. The door was closed and fastened with a padlock.

"I cannot show you that place," said Hanny.

"Do you keep animals inside?" asked Vevi. She was more curious than ever now.

"Not animals," Hanny corrected. "Our cows stay in the barn."

"But what *do* you keep in there, Hanny?" Vevi persisted.

"Vevi!" reproved Connie. She did not consider it good manners to ask so many questions.

"I cannot tell you about the little house," Hanny soberly replied to Vevi's question. "Please—the secret is not mine to relate."

Vevi might have teased a bit. Before she could do so, however, the children were startled to hear loud angry voices. They could not see the speakers, but the sound came from the direction of the house.

"Uncle Peter has lost his temper again!" Hanny gasped. "Oh, dear!"

Gathering up her skirts, she ran swiftly toward the veranda.

Chapter 3

MR. PIFF'S PLAN

VEVI and Connie hastened after Hanny as fast as they could. Breathlessly, the three children reached the veranda where Peter Van Der Lann and Mr. Piff were talking.

"I want no part of it," Mr. Van Der Lann said firmly. "My nursery is not yet profitable. I have no money to donate to your show."

"It will be a money making proposition for you," the promoter argued. "We'll bring folks here to your farm—charge admission. They'll see your fine tulips in bloom and order bulbs. Your business will boom."

"No part of it for me," Mr. Van Der Lann repeated.

At that Mr. Piff again lost patience.

"You are a stubborn Dutchman!" he exclaimed. "You come to America with only one thought—to make money!"

The children thought that Peter meant to strike the promoter, he became so angry. His ruddy face flushed an even darker hue and he drew in his breath sharply.

"You insult me," he said. "Leave my farm! Leave it at once, and don't come back!"

"Okay, okay, Dutchman," Mr. Piff muttered, backing away. "Just keep your shirt on! I meant no offense."

Miss Mohr and Miss Gordon had been deeply distressed by the turn of the conversation. They apologized to Peter, telling him that they did not know Mr. Piff well. They said too, that they were sorry they had brought him to the farm to cause trouble.

"The fault is mine," said Peter, smiling warmly. "It is my hot temper again! You must forgive me. I did not mean to be rude or lacking in hospitality."

"I'm sure you didn't," replied Miss Mohr with a gracious manner. She turned to follow Mr. Piff to the car.

"No, no! You cannot go now!" cried Peter in distress. "First you must have tea and chocolate. Come inside, all of you."

Vevi and Connie eagerly started up the veranda steps. The Brownie Scout leader and Miss Mohr held back, scarcely knowing what to do.

Mr. Piff's Plan

"Mr. Piff is waiting for us," Miss Mohr said uneasily. "We really should go—"

But Peter would not let the meeting end on an unpleasant note. He urged Hanny to take the two women, Vevi and Connie into the parlor. Then he went to the car to tell Mr. Piff he was sorry to have spoken so hastily.

"You'll reconsider and go in with us on the flower show?" Mr. Piff demanded.

Peter shook his head. "No, no!" he said impatiently. "I have told you already—I have no money for such affairs."

"I'll make you change your mind yet," Mr. Piff insisted. "You're missing the chance of a lifetime."

Halfway restored to good humor, he allowed Peter to escort him into the farmhouse.

Miss Mohr, Miss Gordon and the children already had gone inside. Hanny had called the housekeeper, Mrs. Schultz, a plump German lady, who kept the premises as neat as a pin.

"Oh, how delightful!" Miss Mohr exclaimed, her gaze roving over the room.

The walls were half-paneled in oak, with a deep white frieze above for the display of blue Delft ware. A brace of crossed pipes hung above the massive mantel.

The Brownie Scouts at Windmill Farm

All of the furniture was solid, the huge cupboard, the carved chest and the high-back chairs. The wooden floor was so highly polished that Vevi and Connie had to walk carefully not to slip and fall.

While the women admired the Delft tiles and Maiolica ware Peter had brought from Holland, Hanny helped Mrs. Schultz prepare hot chocolate.

Soon the little girl came in with the steaming cups. After that she served tiny little cakes with pink and white frosting.

When finally it was time to leave, Peter cordially invited Miss Mohr, Miss Gordon and the Brownies to come again.

"You'll see me too!" declared Mr. Piff noisily. "I've not given up, Mr. Van Der Lann. Not on your life! The more I see of Windmill Farm the better I like the place. We'll have to include you in our big show, Peter."

Peter merely shook his head and made no reply. It was plain to Vevi and Connie that he did not like Mr. Piff nor his familiar way of calling him "Peter" upon such short acquaintance.

Embarrassed by the promoter's manners, Miss Gordon and the librarian quickly said goodbye. Before leaving, Miss Mohr urged Hanny to come to

Mr. Piff's Plan

the library often. Miss Gordon told the little girl she would be welcome at the next Brownie Scout meeting.

"When will that be?" Hanny asked eagerly.

"The date isn't certain," Miss Gordon replied. "I will have either Connie or Vevi let you know."

As the car started toward Rosedale, the Brownie Scout leader and Miss Mohr could talk of little else than the many beautiful treasures in Peter's home.

"He has a nice place," Mr. Piff admitted grudgingly. "A stubborn fool though!"

"I don't agree with you," Miss Mohr replied. "Surely it is his right to decide whether or not he wants to have a part in a commercial show."

"He'd have gone for it if you had spoken a single favorable word," Mr. Piff went on. "What do you have against me anyhow?"

"Nothing," returned the librarian. She spoke shortly for she had lost all patience with the promoter.

For awhile, Mr. Piff drove in moody silence. Once though, when Vevi lowered the rear window a trifle, he yelled at her to put it up again.

The children decided they never had met a more disagreeable man than the promoter. They were

27

glad, though, that they had made the trip to Windmill Farm, for otherwise they would not have become acquainted with Hanny and her uncle.

"Let's go back there some day after school," Vevi proposed.

"So you can ride in the dog cart again?" teased Connie.

Vevi made a grimace. "I'm not afraid of that old dog!" she insisted. "Next time I'll take a switch and make him obey! I want to see the inside of the old mill."

"So do I, Vevi. Maybe we can go out there again next week, if our mothers will let us."

"Some of the flowers should be in bloom by then," Vevi went on. "I'd like to load the boat with them and float down to the Mattox place."

"And be run off," Connie added with a laugh. "That's you, Vevi, always ready for trouble."

"Why do you suppose the Mattoxes aren't friendly with Peter and Hanny?"

"How should I know?" shrugged Connie. "Maybe it's because they come from Holland. That shouldn't make any difference, though."

Vevi's mind, as active as a humming bird, had darted on.

Mr. Piff's Plan

"Why do you suppose that boat is called the Golden Tulip?" she speculated. "And why wouldn't Hanny tell us what was kept in that padlocked little house?"

"She did act mysterious about it," Connie admitted.

The car sped on, striking an uneven place in the pavement. Vevi was thrown forward in her seat. She would have struck the coat rack had not Miss Gordon reached out to hold her back.

"We're going rather fast," she said pointedly to Mr. Piff.

"Have to get back to town," he replied without slowing down. "I have an appointment at the hotel with a man from the Chamber of Commerce. We stayed too long at Windmill Farm."

The automobile whirled around a bend in the road so fast that the tires screamed. Then Mr. Piff had to put on the brakes.

Directly ahead, was a stalled car. The hood was up and a middle-aged lady in a blue hat, stood looking helplessly at the dead engine.

"Shouldn't we stop and offer to help?" Miss Gordon suggested. "There isn't a garage closer than two miles."

The Brownie Scouts at Windmill Farm

"No time," Mr. Piff muttered. "I'll be late for my appointment. Women shouldn't drive cars if they don't know how to repair them."

"I only hope Mrs. Langley doesn't recognize us as we whirl pass," remarked Miss Mohr.

"Mrs. Langley?" Mr. Piff demanded. "Not the garden club president?"

"Well, yes," nodded the librarian.

"Well, why didn't you say so?" Mr. Piff took his foot from the accelerator and applied the brakes.

Even so, he could not immediately stop the car. It sped past the stalled automobile and pulled up some distance down the road. Mr. Piff started to back up.

"Your appointment—" began Miss Gordon dryly.

"That can wait," Mr. Piff rejoined. "My motto is 'Always help a lady in distress.' Particularly if her name is Mrs. Langley!"

Chapter 4

THE LITTLE LOCKED HOUSE

LEAPING out of the sedan, Mr. Piff rushed over to the stalled automobile to offer his services to Mrs. Langley.

"Having trouble?" he inquired, tipping his hat.

"I think a wire must be broken somewhere," replied Mrs. Langley. "Either that or the fan belt. Oh, dear, I know so little about motors."

"Allow me," said Mr. Piff.

He took off his coat and rolled up his sleeves. But after puttering over the stalled engine for a few minutes, he told Mrs. Langley he was afraid he could not find the trouble.

"Suppose I take you to your destination and send a garageman for your car," he suggested.

"I should be most grateful! I was on my way home when the car suddenly went dead as I rounded the bend. But won't it be too much trouble to drop me off?"

"Not at all," insisted Mr. Piff, escorting the club woman to his own car.

Mrs. Langley knew Miss Gordon and Miss Mohr very well and was pleased to see them again. During the drive to her nearby estate, she chatted gaily of her plans for the coming garden show.

"You're exactly the person I've wanted to see," Mr. Piff told her. "I have a plan which I know will interest you—"

From that point on, he talked and talked, outlining his scheme for the big commercial flower show. At first Mrs. Langley did not seem very much impressed. However, before the ride ended, she had begun to ask many questions.

"Do come in," she invited the group when finally the car reached her home. "You must see my gardens."

"Another time perhaps," said Miss Gordon. "Mr. Piff was in a hurry to keep an appointment—"

"That can wait," he cut in. "Nothing shall deprive me of the pleasure of viewing Mrs. Langley's beautiful garden."

The hour had grown late. Miss Mohr and Miss Gordon felt they should be returning to their homes. However, Mr. Piff had forgotten his haste entirely. To the annoyance of the two women, he insisted upon remaining.

The Little Locked House

The grounds were well-kept and very lovely. Tiny box hedges edged the formal flower beds. There were fountains, a gazing globe and a sun dial.

"How would you children like to pick yourselves a tussie-mussie bouquet?" suggested Mrs. Langley.

"What is that?" asked Vevi, who had never heard of such a thing.

The garden club president explained that a tussie-mussie bouquet really was a tiny nosegay, or flowers arranged for their scents. Each little bouquet was set off with a small paper lace cap.

"You may select any scents you wish," Mrs. Langley said, leading the girls on to another old-fashioned garden. "Lavender—heliotrope—mignonette—rosemary or lemon verbena."

"Say, that tussie-mussie idea is good! Has great commercial possibilities!" exclaimed Mr. Piff. "We could set up a booth and have the Brownies sell them at the flower show!"

"The Brownies are not interested," Miss Gordon said firmly. She had grown increasingly annoyed by the promoter's tactics. "Really, we should be going—"

Mr. Piff ignored the hint. While Vevi and Connie gathered flowers for their tiny bouquets, he kept talking to Mrs. Langley about his wonderful plans for the tulip festival.

"You have one of the finest gardens I ever have seen," he flattered the club woman. "It should be thrown open to the public—for a fee, of course."

"I do open my gardens each year, Mr. Piff," she told him. "However, I have never charged admission."

The visitors were conducted to the greenhouse, where orchids and other tropical plants were grown. Under the glass roof it was so warm that Vevi and Connie were glad to get outside again into the fresh air.

They ran on ahead of the adults to the old wishing well.

"I'm going to make a wish," declared Vevi quickly. "It's about Mr. Piff too!"

She dropped a flower petal down into the water and was very quiet for a moment.

"There!" she announced. "I've made my wish. Now it's your turn, Connie. What will you wish?"

"No fair telling or it won't come true."

"You can give a hint, Connie. That wouldn't do any harm."

"My wish is about Windmill Farm."

The Little Locked House

"You're hoping we can go there again and find out about that locked room!" Vevi instantly guessed. "Isn't that so?"

"Maybe," laughed Connie, dropping her petal into the still water. "I won't tell!"

Just then the grownups came up the path. Mr. Piff seemed in very jubilant spirits. Vevi and Connie soon learned the reason for his good humor. He had won from Mrs. Langley a promise that she would assist financially with the commercial flower show!

The purpose of his visit accomplished, Mr. Piff now was ready to leave. He hustled everyone to the car, and promptly delivered the children to their separate homes.

Connie and Vevi heard no more about the flower show until the next Brownie Scout meeting at the library. Miss Gordon then told the girls that Mr. Piff had talked nearly everyone in Rosedale into cooperating in his scheme.

"Everyone except Peter Van Der Lann," Miss Mohr amended.

"And the Brownies," added Connie with a laugh. "Or will we help too?"

"I have not agreed to let the organization take part," Miss Gordon said. "I feel we should help Mrs.

Langley, but I am opposed to assisting Mr. Piff in his commercial scheme. Somehow, I do not trust him."

"It would be fun though, to sell things in the show," Rosemary Fritche remarked wistfully. "Those tussie-mussie bouquets perhaps."

"Maybe we could have a Brownie booth," Jane Tuttle proposed. "We could wear fancy costumes."

"Dutch dresses and wooden shoes!" cried Vevi. "Maybe Hanny could help us make our costumes!"

"Not so fast, children!" laughed Miss Gordon. "You're miles ahead of me. I don't mind if the Brownies have a booth at the regular garden show, but anything we sell must be for charity."

"May we have a booth?" Connie asked eagerly.

Miss Gordon said she would talk the matter over with Mrs. Langley. She agreed with Vevi that if they did decide to help, it would be nice for the Brownies to wear colorful Dutch costumes.

"Hanny probably can tell us where to get wooden shoes!" Vevi exclaimed. "When will she come to our Brownie meetings?"

"Has anyone given her a definite invitation?" inquired the teacher.

No one had. True, Vevi and Connie had talked

The Little Locked House

with the little girl about joining the troop but they had not told her when the group would meet.

"Why don't we hike out there right now and invite her to our next meeting?" Sunny Davidson proposed. "Anyway, I'd like to see Windmill Farm."

"So would I," declared Rosemary, who had heard a great deal about the nursery from her friends. "May we go right now, Miss Gordon?"

"Well—I had thought we might make scrapbooks this afternoon."

"Can't that wait?" pleaded Vevi. "It's such a nice day for a hike."

"I think so too," agreed Miss Mohr, supporting the girls. "Let's all go."

Windmill Farm was only a short way into the country. The Brownie Scouts enjoyed the walk and made the most of it by noticing birds, flowers and trees as they hiked.

Presently, they came within view of the Dutch windmill. However, it was such a still day that the giant arms hung motionless.

Miss Gordon told the children that in Holland similar windmills were needed to pump water and prevent the sea from flooding lowlands. She explained, too, that the people of The Netherlands love flowers and are noted for raising especially fine tulips.

"Our best bulbs come from there," she declared. "Since Peter Van Der Lann started his nursery here, Rosedale is rapidly becoming a known flower center. Many folks say that his imported bulbs are the best that can be bought anywhere in this country."

"Did you ever hear of a Golden tulip?" Vevi questioned, recalling the name printed on Mr. Van Der Lann's boat.

"There are all types, Vevi. All colors too. Nurserymen constantly are trying to develop new strains."

The driveway was fringed with pink and white dogwood trees which had splattered their petals on the gravel. A big gray sedan stood in front of the little nursery office building.

"Mr. Van Der Lann must have a customer," Miss Mohr remarked.

The nurseryman was talking to a well-dressed woman in a navy-blue suit and fox fur. However, when the Brownie Scouts trooped into the office, he noticed the party at once. He bowed to Miss Gordon and bestowed an especially nice smile upon Miss Mohr.

The Little Locked House

"Just a moment, please," he requested.

While they waited, the Brownies wandered about the office room. Garden tools and seeds were for sale, and there were bins of bulbs and tubers.

Connie and Vevi looked eagerly about for Hanny.

"You should find her at the house," Mr. Van Der Lann advised.

The Brownies dashed off in search of the little Dutch girl. However, at the house, no one answered. The door to the kitchen stood ajar, but not even the housekeeper was there.

"Maybe Hanny is down by the canal," Vevi suggested.

"Or in the cheese house," added Connie.

The two girls enjoyed showing Rosemary, Jane and Sunny over the farm. Because they wanted to keep the secret to themselves, they did not tell the others about the locked door or the mystery connected with it. In passing the little building, though, they noticed that the padlock still was clamped shut.

"Where can Hanny be?" Jane speculated.

"Maybe she is out in the fields," Sunny suggested.

"First, I want to look inside the cheese house," Connie said.

She opened the door of the building to peer inside. The room appeared empty at first glance. Milk had been poured into the pans, but no one was working there.

Connie started to leave. Then she stood very still, listening. She could hear an odd sobbing sound which came from a far corner of the room.

There on an old couch lay Hanny! The little girl was curled kitten-fashion into a tight ball. Her hands covered her face and she was trying desperately to smother her loud sobs.

Chapter 5

HANNY'S SECRET

"WHY, Hanny!" exclaimed Connie, amazed to see the little girl weeping. "What is wrong?"

Hanny had not heard the Brownie Scouts come into the cheese room. She sat up quickly, wiping her eyes and blinking fast.

"Why are you crying?" Vevi asked when she did not answer Connie's question.

Hanny shook her head and turned her face toward the wall. All the Brownies felt very sorry for her.

"Is it because you have to work hard here at the farm?" Connie asked after a moment.

"Oh, no!" Hanny denied, stirred by the question. "I do not work hard."

"Then you must be crying because you never have any fun."

Hanny shook her long yellow braids emphatically. She wiped away the tears and sat up on the couch.

"No, no!" she protested. "You do not understand. I am so very happy here. I love America. I love my so good uncle. Everyone!"

"Then what is wrong, Hanny?"

"I cry because I am sad. My uncle told me today that I may have to go back to my homeland."

"But why?" demanded Jane. "I don't get it."

"My uncle is heavily in debt." sighed Hanny. "He owes much money for this farm and all the what-you-call improvements on it. Now the bank men have told him he must pay."

"Oh, don't you worry," Vevi assured her carelessly. "Everything will turn out all right."

"Not unless my uncle makes money fast," Hanny insisted. "If tulip bulbs only sold for five thousand dollars apiece it would be easy."

"Who ever heard of a bulb selling for that price!" scoffed Jane.

"Oh, but they did at one time," Hanny said. "During the tulip-o-mania bulbs sold for great sums."

"What is a tulip-o-mania?" curiously inquired Sunny.

"I know!" cried Connie before Hanny could answer. "It was a period in Dutch history when the people went crazy over tulips."

Hanny's Secret

"They lost and made fortunes buying and selling them," added Hanny. "I will tell you about it."

Forgetting the cause of her tears, the little Dutch girl began to describe the strange period in history.

She related that in 1634 the entire Dutch population traded in tulip bulbs. At first everyone made money. Tulips kept selling for higher and higher prices.

"Then suddenly, people came to their senses," Hanny went on. "Instead of paying thousands of *florins* for a single bulb, no one wanted them at any price. People lost all their money."

"I hope it won't be that way here," remarked Rosemary anxiously. "My father says that many nurserymen have invested heavily in tulips this year."

"People always will buy tulip bulbs," said Hanny. "But they will not pay high prices any more except for very special bulbs."

"Can't your uncle raise a special bulb?" Vevi questioned. "One that's better than any other tulip in the world?"

Hanny smiled and said she did not think the Brownies knew how difficult it was to develop a fine, new tulip.

"Uncle Peter has one though," she admitted. "If it should catch the fancy of the public, he might yet make his fortune. Then I could stay in America!"

"Does this new tulip have a name?" inquired Connie.

"I gave it one myself," Hanny said proudly.

The Brownies pleaded with her to tell the name, but she would not.

"It's a secret," she insisted. "At least until after the prize is announced."

"Prize?" Vevi asked alertly. "What prize?"

"Mrs. Langley has offered a blue ribbon for the best tulip entered in the show."

"Only a ribbon?" asked Rosemary. "Not a cash prize?"

"The winner of the blue ribbon will earn much money selling the prize bulbs. If the tulip catches the public fancy, the winning grower will receive large orders from all over the country."

"I wish you'd show us the tulip to be entered in the contest," Vevi said.

"It is a secret. No one knows except my Uncle Peter, Bruno and me!"

"Bruno is a dog!" scoffed Vevi. "How can he know?"

"Bruno knows many things," laughed Hanny. "He is a very smart dog. He hauls the milk and at night he keeps people from climbing the fence and stealing our flowers."

"What color is that special tulip?" Vevi demanded. "Is it red?"

"I don't dare tell," laughed Hanny. "Wouldn't the Mattoxes like to know, though!"

"The couple on the next farm?" questioned Connie, recalling mention of the name.

"*Ja*," laughed Hanny, lapsing into a Dutch word. "They are what you call snoops! But they will never learn Uncle Peter's secret!"

To keep the Brownies from asking too many questions about the tulip, the little Dutch girl took them through the old mill. It was exciting indeed to look at all the pulleys and machinery.

Hanny showed the girls a mechanism which acted as a brake. It was used to prevent the mill from pumping too much water into the irrigation ditches.

"It is my job to watch the windmill," Hanny told her friends. "Whenever the wind is too strong, I lock the mechanism."

After the tour had ended, the girls all sat down

on the grass to talk. Connie invited Hanny to attend the next Brownie meeting at the Public Library.

"It will be Wednesday right after school," she said. "Can you come?"

"I think so, but I am not sure," Hanny replied. "It will depend upon my stand."

"A flower stand?" asked Jane.

"Yes, my uncle is letting me have one at the roadside. I will sell bouquets of tulips mostly."

"I'd like to do that myself," Jane declared. "Maybe the Brownies will have a stand at Mrs. Langley's garden show."

"Everything's so mixed up, we don't know what we're supposed to do," Vevi added with a laugh. "We promised Mrs. Langley we would help her with the regular show. Then Mr. Piff came along and talked her into working with him for a bigger festival."

"In my country we call a festival a *kermis*," Hanny said. "You should bake *ellekoek* and sell them!"

"What is that?" asked Jane suspiciously.

"Thin cakes in long, narrow ribbons," Hanny explained with a chuckle. "One sells them by the yard.

Hanny's Secret

In my country, the children buy them at the *kermis* or festival. A child takes each end of the cake. They eat toward each other and kiss at the last bite!"

"How silly!" exclaimed Jane. "I wouldn't like that."

"I'd rather sell flowers," declared Vevi. "Either tulips or tussie-mussie bouquets."

Hanny told the girls she would try very hard to attend the Wednesday Brownie Scout meeting.

"I've told you about Holland," she declared. "Now you must tell me more about the Brownie Scout organization."

"Our motto is 'Be Prepared!'" Sunny explained. "I guess it means learning how to do things well ahead of time, so they can be done right when you're called on to do it."

"You ought to learn the greeting too," Vevi asserted. "When one Brownie Scout meets another, she doesn't just say 'Hi!'"

"You use the sign of friendship." Rosemary took up the explanation. "See, it's done this way."

She held up her first two fingers, stiff and straight, token of the two parts of the Brownie Scout Promise.

"The promise is this," she added: "'I promise to do my best to love God and my country, to help other people every day, especially those at home'."

"I know that part," Hanny declared.

"I guess you help out plenty at home," Connie said. "Do you know the slogan?"

Hanny shook her head.

"It's this: 'Do a Good Turn Daily.'"

"Miss Gordon says that means doing something for someone without being asked or paid for it."

"Things like setting the table for your mother," Rosemary explained. "Or maybe washing the dishes."

"I would like to do something for the Brownies!" declared Hanny. "I know! Next week I will give you some of our tulips. We will have oceans of them in bloom by then."

"You can do something for the Brownies right now," said Connie. "If we have our booth in the flower show, we plan to dress in Dutch costumes. Do you know where we can buy some wooden shoes?"

"Buy sabots?" Hanny echoed. "Why don't you make them?"

"Make our own wooden shoes?" Connie repeated in amazement.

"My uncle does," Hanny said proudly. "He carves

them from wood, with special tools. Maybe he will make shoes for the Brownies!"

"That would be too much trouble," Connie replied quickly.

"If Uncle Peter is not too busy, I think he will do it. I will ask him. First though, before we go to the office, would you like to see our south field? The first tulips are coming into bloom."

Eagerly, the Brownies assented. Hanny walked ahead with Connie and Vevi over the soft ground. Entering through a picket gate, they made their way between seemingly endless rows of bright green plants.

"All of our fields are now in bud," Hanny declared. "We will have a very large flower harvest unless rain or a heavy wind should harm the plants."

"I haven't seen any tulips in bloom except in the greenhouses," Connie remarked.

"Uncle Peter's are the first in Rosedale. The ones in this field are an especially early variety."

"Is the prize tulip here?" Vevi teased.

"I'm not saying," laughed Hanny. "Maybe it is, and maybe it isn't. You will have to discover the answer for yourself."

Already, though not fully in bloom, the field was

speckled with color. Never had the girls beheld so many different types of tulips.

There were rows of tall pink ones, and short, stubby double yellows. Some were variegated with odd markings.

"Wait until the parrot tulips bloom!" Hanny declared proudly. "They have ragged, queer-shaped petals that look like the feathers of a bird!"

"Your uncle's prize tulip isn't a parrot?" Vevi demanded.

"No, it is not a Parrot tulip or a Cottage type," Hanny replied. "I will tell you that much. It is an early bloomer. My uncle developed it from seed."

"Then it must be in this field," Vevi insisted, allowing her gaze to rove over the brilliant mass of flowers. "Is it in bloom now?"

"I can't say," answered Hanny, her eyes twinkling. "But it is the most beautiful tulip I have ever seen."

Everywhere Vevi and the other Brownies saw wonderful flowers. All were so pretty that they could not decide which one was nicer than the others. Jane loved a large flame colored tulip. Sunny's favorite was a tall rose-hued variety with dark throat.

Then unexpectedly, Vevi saw the tulip that held

Hanny's Secret

her eye like a magnet. Only a single flower was in bloom, surrounded by other tulips in bud. Yet the single specimen, each petal perfect, was breath taking.

The flower had a long, straight stem and in color was a pure, golden yellow. Compared to it, all other yellow tulips in the field appeared faded.

"There it is! The one I like best!" cried Vevi.

"It's my choice too," declared Connie.

Hanny smiled in an odd sort of way. She seemed very pleased that her friends liked the tulip.

"This isn't the special tulip, is it?" demanded Rosemary.

Hanny just kept smiling and did not answer.

"Does this flower have a name?" Vevi asked eagerly.

"We call it the 'Golden Beauty.'"

"'The Golden Beauty'," Vevi repeated triumphantly. "That proves it! Your boat has almost the same name! You can't fool us, Hanny! We've discovered the tulip your uncle intends to enter in the prize contest!"

Chapter Six

WOODEN SHOES

HANNY would not admit that Vevi had guessed which tulip her uncle intended to enter in the blue ribbon contest.

All the Brownies clustered about the plant, exclaiming at the beauty of the single bloom.

"The petals look like spun gold!" declared Connie, peering down into the tulip's deep cup.

"This is the tulip your uncle developed, isn't it?" demanded Vevi. She wanted to force Hanny to tell.

However, Hanny only laughed.

Quickly, she led the Brownies on to another section of the field, devoted entirely to purple flowers.

"You may each pick a bouquet of these," she told the girls. "They are the common type of tulips—not special like the others. Next week, you may have all the tulips you can pick."

"Loads and loads of them?" Sunny asked eagerly.

"We'll have more than we can sell," Hanny explained. "Uncle Peter likes to have the blossoms picked off, so that the strength of the bulb will not be sapped."

The little girl told the Brownies that during the next week, hundreds of visitors likely would come to the farm to see the flowers in bloom. Many would order bulbs for fall delivery, selecting the color and type they liked best.

"If Uncle Peter receives many orders, I may be able to stay in America," Hanny declared. "I hope people like the new varieties he has developed."

The little Dutch girl next took the Brownies to an adjoining field, ablaze with rare and splendid colors.

"Uncle Peter calls these his 'Rembrandt' tulips," Hanny said.

"Wasn't Rembrandt a famous painter?" inquired Connie.

"The tulips were named for him because of their beautiful colors," Hanny explained. "When Darwin tulips 'break' into fantastic color combinations, they are called Rembrandts."

"I like this one," declared Rosemary.

She pointed to a tulip which was very exotic appearing with flame-red petals on a white background.

"It is very pretty," said Vevi, "but I like the Golden Beauty much better."

Connie asked Hanny what caused tulips to change color or to "break" as horticulturists called it.

"Uncle Peter says 'breaking' is really a tulip disease, caused by the combined action of two viruses," the little Dutch girl explained. "The flowers change color, but the plant keeps growing normally."

"My, there must be a lot to growing tulips," sighed Sunny.

As the children trooped out of the Rembrandt field, they spied Peter Van Der Lann near the office. He was watering a display of potted plants as he chatted with Miss Mohr and the Brownie Scout leader.

Hanny immediately sought him to ask if he would have time to make wooden shoes for the girls.

The nurseryman put aside his watering can. "And why should I make wooden shoes?" he asked, smiling indulgently at his beloved niece.

"Because the Brownie Scouts need them to wear at Mrs. Langley's flower show. You can't turn them down, Uncle Peter, because they have invited me to be a Brownie too! May I, Uncle Peter?"

Wooden Shoes

Miss Gordon and the librarian already had talked to the nurseryman about his niece joining the organization. So Peter had his answer ready.

"You may join, little Hanny," he declared. "And I will make the shoes."

"It must be done quickly, for the flower show is next week," Hanny said anxiously. "When will you make the shoes, Uncle Hanny?"

"I will take the measurements now," he said. "Run for my tape measure."

Miss Mohr and Miss Gordon protested that the nurseryman was far too busy to take time to carve wooden shoes for the children.

"I will do it at night," he replied. "To whittle wood provides relaxation after a hard day in the fields."

The two young women declared that they would pay for the work. Mr. Van Der Lann would not hear of such a thing. He insisted that the children were Hanny's friends and his, and that it was little enough he could do to show his liking.

Soon Hanny came running back with a tape measure. Peter sat the children on a bench, and one by one, measured their feet.

Carefully, he marked down the figures on a sheet of paper.

The Brownie Scouts at Windmill Farm

"Connie has the largest foot," he reported. "For her shoes I must have a very long piece of white wood."

"What will our shoes look like when they are finished?" asked Rosemary.

"I will show you," Hanny said.

Off she darted to the house again. In a moment she returned, two pairs of wooden shoes tucked under her arms.

The shoes were too small for Connie and Jane, but the other Brownies tried them on. First Sunny tried to walk in them.

Her feet felt very stiff and awkward. After she had taken four steps one of the shoes slipped off.

"You don't do it right," laughed Hanny. "See, I will show you."

She slipped into the shoes which were an exact fit. Instead of walking, she ran across the yard toward the cheese house. The door was open.

One moment the children saw Hanny and her long braids framed in the doorway. The next instant she had disappeared into the building.

But setting neatly by the door were the wooden shoes!

"How did she do that?" cried Vevi in admiration.

Wooden Shoes

"Why, she didn't even slow down when she went through the doorway!"

"I never saw her slip off her shoes," added Jane. "She did it in a flash."

"Hanny learned that trick when she was very young," Peter chuckled. "She did not like to take time to remove her shoes before entering the house, so she learned to take them off on the fly."

Hanny only stayed in the cheese house a moment. Soon she came out to pick up her shoes again.

"Let me see if I can do that!" cried Vevi.

Hanny gave her the shoes, putting on her leather ones again.

"I like these American shoes much better," she said. "Wooden shoes are clumsy."

Vevi slipped into the sabots. She took four little choppy steps and then one of the shoes sailed off.

"I can't run in them at all," Vevi said, very much discouraged.

She went after the shoe which had rolled down a slope toward the canal. Hanny skipped after her to the water's edge.

"I'll show you something else you can do with a wooden shoe," she told the Brownies. "Watch!"

Picking up the wooden shoe that Vevi had lost,

she carefully set it down in the shallow water.

"See, a boat!" she laughed.

The wooden shoe turned slowly around in the sluggish water. Then toe forward, it began to drift lazily away.

"Hey, get it quick!" cried Vevi in alarm.

"Oh, it won't sail far," laughed Hanny.

She was right too, because in just a minute the shoe snagged on a stick and was held fast.

"Say, that's fun, sailing boats!" cried Vevi. "Where is the other shoe?"

"On your foot, stupe!" laughed Jane.

The joke certainly was on Vevi, for in the excitement of watching the "boat" she had forgotten that its mate still was on her left foot.

All the Brownies were eager to play "boat."

"Is it safe?" Miss Gordon anxiously asked the nurseryman.

"Oh, they can't any more than splash their clothing," he replied. "The water barely is deep enough to float the boat."

Reassured, Miss Gordon told the children to have a good time, but to be very careful. She and Miss Mohr then went off with Peter to see some of the tulips.

Connie watched the three walk away. She noticed that the nurseryman seemed especially friendly with Miss Mohr.

"I think he likes her," she whispered to Vevi. "See, he is picking her a bouquet of tulips."

"He likes Miss Gordon too," Vevi replied carelessly. All her attention now had centered on the wooden shoe boats.

"Not the same way though," insisted Connie. "He smiles at her sort of special. Wouldn't it be wonderful if they'd fall in love? Then Hanny could stay here always—"

Vevi gave her friend a sharp jab in the ribs.

"Hush!" she warned. "Do you want Hanny to hear? Anyway, you get crazy ideas, Connie Williams!"

For the next twenty minutes the Brownies had a wonderful time at the water's edge. They peeled off their stockings and sat on the bridge, splashing their toes.

It was great fun sailing the wooden shoes in the lazy current. Now and then a "boat" would fill with water and sink. Then one of the girls would wade to its rescue.

The Brownie Scouts at Windmill Farm

"My shoe is a torpedo boat!" Vevi shouted. "I'm coming after your boat, Jane."

She propelled the shoe, making it crack into the other.

The Brownies played "war" for a few minutes before discovering that the wooden shoes made good sand scoops. Sand castles occupied them after that.

Connie noticed that Miss Mohr, Miss Gordon and Peter had started back from the tulip fields.

"It must be nearly time to leave," she said anxiously. "Vevi McGuire, just look at your dress! What will Miss Gordon say?"

"Yours is splashed too!" Vevi replied, trying to brush off the water drops from her skirt. "It has a spot of mud on the sleeve."

"We'd better quit this game before we get any dirtier," Rosemary declared uneasily. "Let's clean up the wooden shoes."

She gathered up one pair and began to wash out the sand.

Vevi looked about for the other shoes. One lay at the water's edge. The other was nowhere to be seen.

"Connie, did you have Hanny's shoe?" she inquired.

Wooden Shoes

Connie shook her head.

"You had it last," she reminded Vevi. "Remember? When you were playing torpedo."

"I don't recall taking it out of the water," Vevi said, glancing anxiously down the canal. "Did anyone else pick it up?"

No one had seen the shoe.

"It must have drifted away," Hanny said. "Oh, dear, it belonged to my best pair too."

"Where does the canal lead?" Connie questioned.

"Past the Mattox farm and on to a drainage ditch. The shoe couldn't have drifted far though, because the Mattoxes have a footwalk across the water. That would stop the shoe if it went that far."

"Let's go see!" proposed Vevi. She started off toward the adjoining property which was separated from the Van Der Lann place by a tall fence.

"No! No!" Hanny called after her. "We must not trespass."

Vevi did not climb over the fence. But she crawled high up on it so she could see far down the canal.

"I don't see the shoe anywhere," she said, and then she corrected herself. "Oh, yes, I do!"

"Where?" cried Hanny.

"It has snagged on a pile of sticks there where the canal turns a bit!"

Hanny climbed up on the fence beside Vevi. She too saw the runaway shoe.

"I'll run and get it," Vevi offered. She was not afraid to cross the Mattox land.

"No, no!" Hanny said in earnest protest. "Uncle Peter has told me that I must never set foot on their property. They are so very unpleasant."

"Then how will we get the shoe?" Vevi demanded.

Hanny thought hard for a second and then had an idea.

"The watercourse belongs to everybody," she declared. "I will take the boat and fetch the shoe!"

Chapter Seven

A RUNAWAY 'BOAT'

VEVI and Connie offered to go with Hanny to recover the missing wooden shoe. They thought it odd, however, that the Mattox couple should be so strict about anyone walking on their land.

"Is it safe to go in the boat?" questioned Connie as the children walked back to the canal.

"Oh, yes, the water isn't deep," Hanny replied. "I will get the oars."

She ran to the barn, returning with them in a moment. Then she untied the boat and climbed in.

All of the Brownies were eager for a ride on the canal. Hanny though, could not take everyone.

"Vevi and Connie spoke first," she said. "So I will take them."

The two Brownies stepped into the boat with their armful of tulip blooms. By this time the flowers had wilted a bit. Vevi dipped the stems into the canal for a moment and then put the bouquets on the bottom of the boat.

As she bent down she noticed that a little water was seeping in through the boards.

"Say, I think this old boat is leaking!" she cried.

"It always does a little," Hanny replied, picking up the oars.

Vevi and Connie moved their feet so that their shoes would not get wet.

"Shove us off," Hanny urged the Brownies who had remained ashore.

Jane gave the boat a mighty push. Out it shot into the current. For a moment, before slowing down, the craft went almost as fast as if it had a motor.

"Say, this is fun!" shouted Vevi.

Jane, Rosemary and Sunny ran along the bank beside the boat. When they reached the fence that separated Mr. Van Der Lann's property from the Mattox farm, they had to stop.

Hanny began to row. She handled the oars very well and kept the boat steady in the middle of the canal.

"Say, this old boat is leaking fast!" Vevi observed very soon. "My feet are getting wet."

"So are mine," declared Connie, shifting to another place in the boat.

A Runaway 'Boat'

Hanny told Vevi to look for a bailing can under the seat. The container could not be found.

"I remember, I used it for something else last week and forgot to put it back," Hanny admitted.

Vevi and Connie began to squirm nervously. The water was not deep but it kept spreading over the bottom of the boat.

"I want out of this old tub," Vevi suddenly announced. "It is going to sink!"

Hanny insisted that the boat was safe. "I can't let you out because we are at the Mattox place now," she added. "We will soon have that runaway shoe and be back home."

Vevi and Connie forgot the leaking boat as they looked about with interest. From the Van Der Lann place tall trees and bushes had screened their view of the other nursery.

Now they saw the big greenhouse with its glass roof and a small cottage very much in need of paint. A few tulips were in bloom, but the flowers were not as large or as showy as those on Peter's place.

"The Mattoxes lived here before my uncle started his nursery," Hanny told her friends. "They were annoyed when he bought land next to their property. They had expected to add it to their own place."

"Is that Mrs. Mattox?" Connie asked. She had noticed a woman in a blue straw hat working in the fields.

"Her name is Freda," Hanny said. "If she sees us, she may speak crossly. She does not like me or Uncle Peter."

"Say, my feet are wet!" Vevi suddenly cried.

"The water is coming into this boat faster and faster," Connie declared uneasily. "Hanny, you must pull up on shore."

"Mrs. Mattox won't like it."

"Who cares about her?" Vevi demanded. "We are getting wet, Hanny."

The little Dutch girl guided the boat to a sandy stretch of beach along the canal. After Connie and Vevi had leaped out, she pulled the craft up on shore so it would not drift away.

"Mrs. Mattox has seen us," Hanny said, glancing over her shoulder. "Oh! Oh! She has dropped her hoe and is coming this way."

"Let's get the wooden shoe as fast as we can and run!" Vevi urged.

Abandoning the boat, the children ran to the clutter of debris where the runaway shoe had caught fast.

A Runaway 'Boat'

But when Connie tried to capture it, she only succeeded in setting it free. Off it floated again down the canal.

"Hey, come back here, shoe!" she cried.

The "boat" drifted lazily along until finally it lodged against a footbridge.

"Now we can get it," declared Vevi.

"And Mrs. Mattox will get us," added Hanny nervously. "She is walking straight to our boat."

The children walked quickly out on the footbridge. The narrow planking bent under their weight and dipped low into the water.

"It's going to break!" Vevi exclaimed fearfully.

"Oh, a footbridge always wobbles," Connie reassured her. "Here, hold my hand while I grab the old shoe."

Vevi steadied her so she could bend down and rescue the shoe.

"Now back to the boat!" Hanny urged. "We are going to get a scolding, I can tell you."

Mrs. Mattox did not pay very much attention to the three girls as they hurried up the canal. In fact, she seemed deeply engrossed examining something in the bottom of the boat.

"What is she doing?" Vevi asked curiously.

The Brownie Scouts at Windmill Farm

"Maybe she is trying to stop the leak in our boat," Connie speculated.

Hanny however, had sharper eyes.

"She is looking at our tulips," she told her companions. "Just see her poking about among the blossoms."

"Why would she do that?" Vevi whispered. By this time the children had drawn quite close to the boat.

"She's trying to see what varieties Uncle Peter is raising this year," Hanny declared. "I think she is hoping to find out if we have a tulip that will win the blue ribbon."

Mrs. Mattox had heard the children come up. She straightened, dropping a red tulip.

For a minute the girls thought she intended to scold them for coming onto her property. Instead, she merely stared at them.

"Our boat is leaking," Hanny said politely. "That is why we walked on your land."

"It isn't the first time you have done it," the woman answered. She kept eyeing the tulips in the boat.

"Hanny gave us some flowers," Connie said to

A Runaway 'Boat'

make conversation. She always tried to be friendly with everyone. "Aren't they beautiful?"

"Humph! Very ordinary tulips I would say," replied Mrs. Mattox. "Which one is your uncle entering in the flower show, Hanny?"

"I cannot say, Mrs. Mattox."

"None of these, I'd judge."

Hanny remained silent. Her unwillingness to talk angered the woman.

"How many times have I told you not to come onto my property?" she berated the children. "You tramp the flowers and damage our plantings."

Hanny knew the accusations were unfair. It was true, though, that she had been told repeatedly not to trespass.

"We are leaving now," she said.

"Take this leaky old tub with you," Mrs. Mattox ordered crossly. "You will have to tow it back by the rope because it is becoming waterlogged. Now, begone!"

Hanny seized the rope and started to pull the boat alongshore. Mrs. Mattox followed close behind to see that she did not do any damage.

"I am sorry about the boat," Hanny apologized

again. "My uncle plans soon to build a new one."

"Such foolishness!" the nurseryman's wife exclaimed. "First it was a windmill! What will it be next? Always foolishness."

"I like the windmill," Vevi said, speaking in Peter's defense. "His farm is very pretty. It is nicer than this one."

Now the little girl should not have made the remark. She was sorry the moment she had said the words. Mrs. Mattox lost her temper at once.

"Oh, so Peter Van Der Lann has a better nursery than ours!" she exclaimed. "Well, let me tell you something! He won't have it long. Everyone in Rosedale knows that he is deeply in debt. He will lose his farm, and then where will he be?"

Chapter 8

THE TREASURE HOUSE

MRS. Mattox' words distressed Hanny, who began to cry. She knew only too well that her uncle might lose his property and that she would be sent back to Holland.

"My uncle won't lose his farm," she denied stubbornly. "He will make a great deal of money this year. Our tulip will win the prize and we will sell our bulbs for a nice price."

"Don't count on it," said Mrs. Mattox. "Your uncle will win no prize with any of the tulip varieties I have seen."

"We have one though—" Hanny began, and then she stopped short. She realized she had been on the verge of saying too much.

"Where does your uncle grow this wonderful tulip?" Mrs. Mattox pursued the subject.

Hanny would not say. She was glad when they reached the boundary of her uncle's land. The other

Brownies were at the fence and helped to pull the water-logged boat back to its mooring place.

"Don't you mind Mrs. Mattox," Connie said to Hanny, slipping an arm about the little girl's waist. "She is just an old meanie."

"But it is true my uncle may lose this farm."

"You will win the blue ribbon for your prize tulip."

"I hope so," Hanny said soberly, "but Uncle Peter says we cannot count on it. All the growers in Rosedale are trying for the prize. Many new varieties wil be shown."

"Yours will be the very best," Connie declared confidently. "If it is the Golden Beauty I am sure it will win."

The children hauled the leaky boat up on the grassy bank. As they overturned it, Miss Gordon hailed them from the path.

"Come to the house, girls," she called. "Mr. Van Der Lann has invited us to have sweet cakes."

"I'll give you some of my *hopjes* too," declared Hanny.

"What are those?" Jane Tuttle asked as the group started for the house. "Something to eat?"

"Candy with a butterscotch flavor," Hanny explained. "Good too!"

The Treasure House

Inside the farm house, Peter had laid a fire on the hearth to take a chill from the air. Hanny, Vevi and Connie moved in close to dry their damp shoes and stockings.

As the children were telling Mr. Van Der Lann about the leaky boat, the housekeeper came in bearing steaming chocolate and *maastegles* or sweet cakes.

While they nibbled the cakes, the grownups talked of the coming flower show. Judging of the tulips, the first event in the mammoth festival, was to come the following weekend. Mrs. Langley planned to open her estate to the public according to her usual custom. Prize flowers would be on display at her greenhouse.

"Mr. Piff keeps at me to have a part in the commercial show," Mr. Van Der Lann said. "To participate I must pay one hundred dollars. I do not have it and have told him so. Yet he has told about Rosedale that I have refused only because I am stubborn."

"From what I hear, many of the growers are regretting that they went into Mr. Piff's scheme," remarked Miss Mohr. "It is to be an elaborate affair and no doubt will bring hundreds of persons to

Rosedale during show week. But some folks are saying that for all his talk, Mr. Piff is not a good manager."

"I have heard rumors myself," nodded Mr. Van Der Lann. "Some of the growers complain that for every dollar Mr. Piff colects, fifty cents goes into his own pocket."

"I liked our festival so much when it was a small, quiet affair," added Miss Gordon. "For the life of me I cannot understand why Mrs. Langley became interested in Mr. Piff's scheme."

The Brownies had just finished their cake when the housekeeper came in. She spoke quietly to the nurseryman.

"Mrs. Gabriel is here again," she informed him. "It is about those bulbs she asked you to order for her."

Mr. Van Der Lann went to the window and looked out. He could see the lady's car on the driveway near the little office.

"Why does she keep pestering me?" he demanded. "I have told her repeatedly that I want none of her business. Tell her I will not see her!"

The Brownies could not understand why the nurseryman did not like to deal with Mrs. Gabriel. Her unexpected visit seemed to upset him.

A little later, when the children were outside again, Vevi asked Hanny why her uncle turned down Mrs. Gabriel's order.

"I do not know," Hanny answered with a shrug.

"Who is she anyhow?" Connie questioned. She did not know anyone in Rosedale by the name of Gabriel.

"She has been here several times," Hanny told her friends. "Always she is nice to me and once gave me a chocolate bar. But I do not like her. Uncle Peter says she is trying to get him to do something he does not want to do."

It was nearly time to leave now, so the children went down to the canal for their bouquets of flowers.

Sunny, Jane and Rosemary quickly gathered up their tulips and carried them back to the house. Vevi and Connie followed more slowly, stopping a moment to watch the revolving arms of the big windmill.

"Hanny," said Vevi suddenly, "when are you going to tell us about the mystery house?"

Hanny grinned and pretended not to understand.

"You know what I mean," Vevi said pointedly. "When are you going to tell us what you keep in that locked building?"

"Someday," Hanny laughed.

"We may not get out here again very soon," Vevi argued. "Next week is the flower show at Mrs. Langley's estate."

"And right after that the big commercial festival," added Connie. "The Brownies will be very busy next week too. We have to make our booth and cut paper tulips to decorate the library."

"But you will have to come again, if only to try on the wooden shoes Uncle Peter is making for you," Hanny protested.

"We won't be able to stay long next time," Vevi insisted. "If you're ever going to tell us about that locked house, now is the time to do it."

Hanny hesitated a long while. Then she demanded:

"Can you both keep a secret?"

"Oh, yes!" said Connie.

"A Brownie's word is as good as gold," added Vevi. "Tell us your secret, Hanny."

"It belongs to Uncle Peter as much as to me. You're sure you can keep the secret if I tell you?"

The Treasure House

"Brownie's honor," said Connie soberly.

"Then wait here," directed Hanny. "I will be back in a minute."

She ran off to the house. Vevi and Connie could not imagine what she was after. Soon she came flying back, something clutched in her hand.

She opened her fingers to show Connie and Vevi that the object was a tiny padlock key.

"Come with me," she bade her friends. "But you must never, never tell what I am going to show you. Not until after next week at least. Then it will not matter."

Connie and Vevi became rather excited at the thought of seeing inside the locked house. They could not guess what Hanny's uncle kept hidden there. It made them feel very important to think that Hanny trusted them enough to let them share her secret.

"We must hurry," Connie said, glancing anxiously toward the house. "I think Miss Gordon and Miss Mohr are about ready to start home."

Hanny inserted the key into the padlock and pulled it open.

"You mustn't tell anyone—not even the other Brownies," Hanny warned.

The Brownie Scouts at Windmill Farm

"We promise," Vevi said impatiently.

Hanny pushed open the door and stepped into the dark room. The other two girls followed quickly behind her.

"I can't see a thing!" Vevi complained.

"Neither can I," declared Connie, clinging to her friend's arm.

"Wait! I will let in a little light," Hanny said. "But only a little."

The room in which the children stood was nearly square, with walls scarcely more than ten feet in length. There were no windows, only a small skylight overhead. The latter had been covered with a blanket to keep out the sunshine.

Hanny moved the covering so that a crack of light filtered down.

"There!" she exclaimed. "Now can you see?"

Vevi and Connie looked about them. The walls of the room were lined with homemade shelves on which were stored large, plump objects which were difficult to identify in the shadowy light.

"Onions!" Vevi exclaimed, finally making out their shape.

She was bitterly disappointed. For that matter, so was Connie.

The Treasure House

"Not onions," corrected Hanny. "Look again."

"Tulip bulbs?" Connie asked.

"Yes," Hanny acknowledged. "Our very best ones are kept here. The temperature is carefully controlled. Uncle Peter and I call this place our treasure house."

Connie and Vevi were so disappointed they could not say a word.

For days they had been speculating about the mystery of the little locked house. They had convinced themselves that this room contained something very startling and wonderful. And now to learn that it was only a storeroom for bulbs!

Hanny seemed to sense how her friends felt. At any rate, she chuckled as if enjoying their astonishment.

"Now, I'll show you the real treasure," she promised. "Then you will understand why the secret must be kept."

Chapter 9

HIGH WIND

MOVING to a shelf on the north wall, Hanny pulled out a canvas bag.

"Not money?" gasped Vevi. Her interest in the locked room had revived quickly.

"This bag contains something which may be as valuable as gold," Hanny replied. "It all depends on whether or not Uncle Peter is lucky."

The little Dutch girl unfastened the bag and carefully emptied out some of the contents on the counter.

"More tulip bulbs!" exclaimed Vevi. "Big ones too."

She had never seen such large bulbs. Each one was plump and perfectly formed. Even Vevi who did not know anything about flower bulbs could see that these were something very fine.

"Are these the special bulbs your uncle developed Hanny?" shrewdly guessed Connie. "Are they the blue ribbon ones?"

"They're the bulbs Uncle Peter hopes will win the prize."

"Why do you keep them locked up?" questioned Vevi.

"Because they will be worth their weight in gold if our tulip wins first prize," Hanny explained. "There are no other bulbs like these anywhere in this country or abroad. Uncle Peter says they are the finest in the world! If we should lose them or if they should rot, we never could replace them."

"Are they bulbs of the Golden Tulip?" Vevi asked.

"I cannot say," returned Hanny. "I would like to tell, but I promised Uncle Peter not to give away the secret."

"The Golden Tulip is the most beautiful one I have seen anywhere," Vevi insisted. "I think these must be Golden Tulip bulbs."

Hanny only laughed and put away the bag. Then she carefully locked the little house again.

"I wish the Brownies had a tulip bed," said Connie after the padlock had been snapped shut. "Miss Mohr might give us a little plot of ground at the library."

The Brownie Scouts at Windmill Farm

"It is too late to start a tulip bed this spring," Hanny advised her. "Bulbs should be planted in the fall."

"Then perhaps the Brownies can have a garden next year. Only then Rosedale may not be having a flower festival."

"Next year, if Uncle Peter still has his nursery, I will give you hundreds of bulbs," Hanny promised.

As the children turned away from the little house, they were startled to hear Jane calling to them from the roadway.

"Hey, hurry up!" she shouted. "We've been waiting nearly ten minutes! Hurry!"

Vevi and Connie hastily said goodbye to Hanny, reminding her not to forget the scheduled Brownie Scout meeting at the library. Then they ran off to join their friends who were ready to start home.

"Say, where did you girls go anyhow?" Jane demanded suspiciously as Vevi and Connie rushed up breathlessly.

"It's a secret," chuckled Vevi.

All the way home, the other Brownies teased her to reveal where she and Connie had been. But Vevi would not.

High Wind

Not until they were alone again, did the two girls so much as mention the locked room.

Both were hopeful that Peter would win the blue ribbon and that his bag of precious bulbs truly would become a bag of treasure.

On Wednesday after school all the Brownie Scouts gathered at the public library to cut and paste tulip decorations for the windows.

"Where is Hanny?" Rosemary asked noticing that the little girl was not present. "I thought she was coming today."

"So did I," declared Miss Gordon. "Perhaps she will come later."

A door banged just then and in came Hanny. She was quite breathless from hurrying.

"I am sorry to be late," she apologized. "I did not think I could come at all. My uncle was called away and there is no one at home to look after things. Even the housekeeper is away."

Miss Gordon said she was happy indeed that Hanny had managed to attend the meeting. She gave the little girl materials and showed her how to make paper flowers.

As the children worked with scissors and paste,

The Brownie Scouts at Windmill Farm

Miss Mohr told them about the work of Brownies in foreign countries.

"Now who remembers the Brownie name in the Netherlands?" she asked the group.

Sunny Davidson and Connie Williams both waved their hands. Miss Mohr called on Sunny to give the answer.

"They're called Kabouters and it means little elves."

"Now who knows the name that is used for the organization in South Africa?" the librarian went on.

No one knew the answer so Miss Mohr told the girls that Brownies in South Africa were known as Sunbeams.

She said that in Greece they were called Poulakia or Little Birds.

Miss Gordon then told the Brownies about cut-out dolls they could obtain. She explained that the figures were dressed in Brownie uniforms of different countries in the World Association of Girl Guides and Girl Scouts.

"Now you know that tulip bulbs came to this country from Holland," she declared. "Look about in your homes, and at our next meeting report how

High Wind

many objects you have noticed that have been imported from other countries."

"Our home has almost everything from Holland," Hanny said. "But I like best the things you buy in America. I love your big super markets too where you see so many wonderful foods."

So that the little girl would know more about the organization she intended to join, Miss Gordon explained how the Brownies obtained their name in English speaking countries.

"The organization was named by Robert Baden-Powell, who lived in England," she told Hanny. "He knew many wonderful stories about the brownies or 'little people' and thought it would be a suitable name for girls who try to be useful. The founder of the Girl Scouts in America was Mrs. Juliette Gordon Low."

"How can I join?" Hanny asked eagerly. "I want to be a Brownie."

"We will have the investiture ceremony as soon as you have attended four meetings," Miss Gordon promised.

After the paper flowers had been made, the girls talked over plans for a booth at Mrs. Langley's flower show. Miss Mohr announced that Peter Van

Der Lann had promised the troop all the tulips they wanted, not only for decoration, but to sell. The mothers would help too, particularly in the making of tussie-mussie bouquets.

"I think the festival on Mrs. Langley's estate will be very nice," Miss Mohr told the girls. "The Brownies will wear Dutch costumes, and wooden shoes. All the money we make will be for our own organization."

It was after four-thirty when the meeting finally came to an end. Vevi and Hanny were among the last to leave the library. Arm in arm they walked along the street together.

"I am going to like being a Brownie," Hanny told her new friend. "Why, I hope I can attend every single meeting."

The children were passing a drugstore window. Vevi stopped to look at a poster which advertised the coming festival. The placard did not mention the preliminary show on Mrs. Langley's estate but told about the three-day celebration which would follow.

Vevi was reading the poster when a sudden gust of wind whipped her Brownie uniform about her knees.

High Wind

At the same instant off went her brown beanie into the gutter.

"Whoops!" Vevi exclaimed, scampering after the rolling headgear.

As she snatched the beanie from the street an automobile came to a jerky halt at the curb. The strange woman Vevi knew as Mrs. Gabriel was at the wheel. She tooted her horn and glared at the little girl.

"Don't you know better than to dash out into the street!" she scolded. "I might have run you down."

Vevi had been a little careless. However, she never had come very close to the automobile.

"I am sorry," she apologized. "That wind—"

Off went her beanie again, this time almost directly beneath the wheels of the stationary car. To the annoyance of Mrs. Gabriel, Vevi had to get down on her hands and knees to fish it out.

"Do watch what you are doing," the woman said. "And hang onto that hat!"

The moment Vevi was safely on the curb, she drove away.

Hanny had been having a time with her own belongings. The capricious wind had scattered some of her school papers. For several minutes she was kept busy gathering them up.

Breathlessly the two girls huddled in the drugstore doorway. As yet there was no rain but dust was blowing wildly in the street. A newspaper flew past, plastering itself around a telephone pole.

"It's going to blow real hard," Vevi said, pulling her sweater tight. "Hanny, you had better come home with me."

"I can't," the other replied. "O-oh!"

Vevi looked around quickly, wondering what was wrong. She thought dust had blown into Hanny's eyes or that another paper had been swept away.

"What is it?" she asked for her little friend looked dreadfully worried.

"The windmill!" Hanny said in a frightened voice. "I left it turned on. If it pumps very long in this high wind, our tulips may be ruined!"

Chapter 10

IN THE HAYLOFT

THE wind was blowing steadily now, whipping the trees and sending everyone to cover.

Hanny and Vevi huddled in the drugstore doorway, not knowing what to do.

"I should have locked the windmill before I left the farm," Hanny said, clutching her hat tightly to keep it from sailing away.

"Maybe your uncle will get home and take care of it," Vevi said hopefully.

"He has gone away for the afternoon. 'Oh, Vevi, I will have to get out there as fast as I can. This wind is not going to let up for a long while."

"I will go with you," Vevi offered. She did not really want to go. It was a long walk to the farm and the sharp wind would make the trip uncomfortable.

Nevertheless, she started off with Hanny down

the street. The girls had to duck their heads and bend low. Even then it was hard to keep on their feet.

"This is a regular hurricane!" Vevi gasped. "Maybe everything is going to blow away!"

Hanny however, was not frightened. She glanced at the sky, studying the boiling clouds for a minute.

"It is only a hard wind," she said. "But it can do much damage at our nursery. Oh, why did I forget the windmill?"

Reaching the outskirts of the city, the two girls struck out along the main highway. Soon they saw a car overtaking them.

"Here comes someone," Vevi said, looking over her shoulder. "Maybe we can catch a ride to the farm."

The children moved off the roadway and waited. When the car was fairly close they could see a woman at the wheel. There were no passengers.

"It looks like Mrs. Gabriel's car," said Hanny. "My uncle would not want me to ride with her."

"Even to save the tulips?"

"I guess that would be different," Hanny agreed.

Both girls waved their arms, trying to attract Mrs. Gabriel's attention. They knew she saw them, for she slowed down.

In the Hayloft

"She is going to pick us up!" Vevi cried in relief.

But Mrs. Gabriel did not stop. She drove past the children, without paying any attention to their frantic gestures.

"Why, that was mean!" exclaimed Vevi. "She'll be going right past the farm too!"

The girls bored on into the wind, but walking was most difficult. Vevi could not keep on her beanie. She carried it in her hand, but her hair kept whipping across her eyes.

"We'll never get there!" she gasped. "This hateful old wind!"

A loud "toot-toot" sounded directly behind the girls. Startled, they jumped to the side of the road.

Another car had come along, driven by a man who was riding with his wife. He pulled up beside the children.

"Want a ride?" he asked.

"Do we!" demanded Vevi gratefully.

The man opened the car door, and the girls slid into the back seat.

"Going far?" he inquired.

"Only to Windmill Farm," Hanny said. "Can you take us there?"

"Sure thing," the man agreed. "I'm going right past the farm."

The car rolled over a bridge. Vevi and Connie saw that the river had been ruffled into high, foamy waves. Along each shore, the lowbent branches of willows were lashing back and forth.

A few big drops of rain spattered against the car's windshield.

"We'll have a downpour any minute now," the driver said. "You children should have your raincoats."

The car passed the Mattox nursery. On the driveway, Vevi and Hanny saw Mrs. Gabriel's parked automobile.

"Look at the roof of the greenhouse!" Hanny cried, pointing.

A portion of the glass covering had been smashed by the wind.

"It was a little twister all right," declared the man who had given the children a ride. "The worst is over now though, I think."

"I hope our windmill is all right," Hanny said anxiously. "It may have blown down."

The car rolled over a rise, and the children were reassured to see the huge canvas-arms revolving at a furious rate.

In the Hayloft

"It's still there," Vevi said, greatly relieved.

"But see how fast the arms are turning," Hanny declared. "The tulip fields will be flooded!"

At the gate to Windmill Farm, the driver stopped the car to let the children off.

"Will you be all right now?" he asked. "Or do you want me to come with you?"

"I can turn off the windmill myself," Hanny said.

She and Vevi thanked the driver and his wife for the ride and ran through the gate.

The windmill was groaning and straining under the assault of the elements. At any moment, Vevi expected to see the canvas-covered arms ripped to shreds.

Around and around went the fan-shaped sails, pumping water at a fearful rate. The irrigation ditches were flooded and Hanny could see that some of the tulip fields were soaked.

"I must get the mill stopped first of all!" she cried.

The little Dutch girl ran to the mill and tried to open the door. The wind held it back.

"Help me, Vevi!" she cried.

Both girls tugged at the door. Vevi lost her beanie again, and this time she did not try to save it.

Suddenly the mill door flew back, banging hard. The wind was so strong it nearly wrenched off the hinges.

Once inside the mill, the girls were protected. But it was frightening to hear the wild creak of the pulleys and the heaving and groaning of the great sails overhead.

"Oh, Hanny, I'm scared," Vevi whimpered, huddling against a wall. "This old mill is about ready to blow over."

Hanny was not as nervous as her little friend, for she had been inside the mill before on very windy days.

Quickly, she shot levers into place, locking the mechanism.

"There, I have stopped the mill from pumping!" she exclaimed.

The girls caught their breath, looking out over the fields through the open doorway.

"This wind will snap the stems of our tulips even if the water did not ruin them," Hanny said. "Uncle Peter will lose most of his investment."

"The wind is dying down some now," Vevi said. "Maybe the tulips will be all right."

In the Hayloft

"I am especially worried about the north field," Hanny went on. "If the prize tulip is lost, we will have nothing to enter in Mrs. Langley's show."

"The Golden Beauty?"

Hanny did not answer. She seemed to be thinking hard.

Suddenly, without explaining what she intended to do, she bolted out the open door of the mill.

Vevi saw the little girl run to the barn. She was inside a minute or two. Then out she came, carrying a large, empty orange crate.

"Where are you going, Hanny?" Vevi shouted across the yard.

In the high wind, Hanny could not hear. But Vevi saw her enter the north field and dart down the rows of tulips.

Hanny carefully set the crate down. Then she came flying back to rejoin Vevi in the mill.

"Our tulip is still safe!" she exclaimed. "I have covered it with the box. Now it will be protected even if the other tulips are ruined."

Vevi had noticed the place where Hanny had set down the box.

"It was the Golden Beauty that you covered,"

she said. "I am sure of it, Vevi. But I will never tell."

The old mill was a chilly and uncomfortable place in which to stand. Hanny said that the barn, directly across the yard, was a much better shelter from which to watch the storm.

"Let's make a run for it," she urged. "The rain is coming."

Together the girls dashed across the open space. Midway there, Vevi spied her lost beanie snagged against a fence post. She darted aside to rescue it. Before she could reach the barn, rain began to come down in torrents.

"Hurry! Hurry!" Hanny shouted, holding the barn door open for her.

Vevi dashed in, her Brownie uniform splashed with raindrops.

For several minutes the rain came in a great sheet. Then abruptly, it let up.

"At least we will not have hail," Hanny declared. "That is what ruins the plants."

Now that the excitement was nearly over, Vevi became interested in the interior of the barn. She had never seen such a clean place.

The floor was swept as neatly as a living room. Curtains were at all the windows. The stalls, where

In the Hayloft

two Jersey cows contentedly chewed their cuds, did not have a speck of dust or dirt.

Vevi sniffed the air. She could smell something sweet and fragrant.

"What is that odor?" she asked.

"The haymow," Hanny told her. "See, the ladder leads up to it."

Vevi climbed up to look. "My, this hay looks nice and soft," she called down.

The little girl suddenly realized that the trip from Rosedale and so much running and hurrying had made her very tired. She snuggled down into a mound of hay.

Hanny also climbed the ladder. Seeing Vevi so snug, she curled up beside her.

The hay was warm and delightful.

"I'm sleepy," Vevi said. "I think I will take a nap. By the time I wake up, the rain will be over."

"It is almost over now," said Hanny.

"I think I will take a nap anyhow," Vevi declared. "Wake me up when it stops raining."

Now Hanny did not intend to fall asleep. After Vevi had closed her eyes, she lay very still listening to the rain on the barn roof.

The hay was sweet-smelling and as cozy as a

feather bed. She felt delightfully drowsy, shut off from all the world.

Hanny thought she would close her eyes only for a moment. When she opened them, she was astonished to see that dark shadows shrouded the haymow.

Vevi was shaking her.

"M-m," Hanny mumbled drowsily. For a moment she could not think where she was or what had happened.

Vevi pressed a hand over Hanny's lips.

"Sh!" she warned.

By this time Hanny had come two-thirds awake. She saw Vevi sitting beside her, hay sticking in her mussed hair.

"Listen!" Vevi whispered.

The rain had ceased and Hanny no longer could hear the whistle of the wind around the corners of the barn. How long had she slept?

Hanny sat up, rubbing her eyes. Only then did she hear a strange murmuring sound from the lower floor of the barn.

"What is that?" she whispered.

"Someone is down there," Vevi answered, very

In the Hayloft

low. "When I woke up, I heard two people talking."

"Maybe it is Peter come home."

"I don't think so Hanny. Besides, there are two people."

Their curiosity aroused, the two girls crept to the edge of the hay loft. Peering down they saw a man and a woman standing in the doorway of the barn.

"It is Mrs. Mattox and her husband Joseph," Hanny whispered. "But why are they here? They refuse me permission to walk on their property."

Mrs. Mattox was cleaning mud from her shoes.

"We should not stand here," her husband said. "Peter Van Der Lann may return at any moment, or his little girl."

"Let them," said the wife. "At any rate, it was your idea to visit his fields to see what the stubborn Dutchman is raising. Now that you have looked under the box are you satisfied?"

"The tulip is superior to anything that we can enter in the show."

"I don't agree," Mrs. Mattox replied. "Our own flower the cherry-rose candy stick tulip is its equal. We will win the prize, Joseph."

The Brownie Scouts at Windmill Farm

"Don't count on it," Mr. Mattox said gloomily.

"We won't need to win the blue ribbon to have a profitable business. We have valuable customers. Mrs. Gabriel—"

"How many times must I ask you not to mention her name?" Mr. Mattox broke in angrily. "I wish I had never seen her—she may yet be the cause of me going to jail."

"Jail?" his wife echoed. "Joseph, I fail to understand you. When Mrs. Gabriel first came to talk to you, why you said we would make a mint of money. Didn't she give you a large order of bulbs to be imported from Holland?"

"Yes, and I wish she hadn't! Don't forget that woman went first to Peter Van Der Lann with her proposition. He must suspect what is going on. If he should turn me in we both might be jailed."

In the hayloft, Hanny and Vevi caught nearly all of the conversation. But they did not understand why Mr. Mattox was so angry at his wife for mentioning Mrs. Gabriel's name.

Hanny made up her mind she would tell her Uncle Peter all about it when he came home.

"The rain has stopped," she heard Mr. Mattox say. "We can go now."

In the Hayloft

Never guessing that anyone had listened to their talk, the couple left the barn. By the time Vevi and Hanny had slid down from the loft, they were nowhere in sight.

Chapter 11

THE MAN IN GRAY

WHEN Peter Van Der Lann drove into the farm yard twenty minutes later, Hanny and Vevi ran to meet him.

"I came as fast as I could," the farmer said. "Is everything all right?"

Finding English inadequate, Hanny spoke rapidly in Dutch, telling him everything that had happened during his absence.

Mr. Van Der Lann did not have much to say until he had inspected the tulip fields. Although the high wind and rain had flattened many of the plants, they were not as badly damaged as he had feared.

"Now that the sun is coming out again, they will straighten up," he said. "We will have a good flower harvest, Hanny."

The nurseryman did not scold his niece for having forgotten about the windmill. Instead, he told her

The Man in Gray

that she probably had saved the tulip field by shutting off the water.

"As for Mr. and Mrs. Mattox," he said indifferently, "give them no thought, little Hanny."

"But Uncle Peter, they came while you were away to peep under the box!"

"It does not matter. Before this week has ended, everyone will have seen our beautiful tulip."

"Mrs. Mattox spoke of a tulip they are entering in the show, Uncle Peter. A cherry-rose candy stripe, she called it."

"It will not compare with our flower," declared Mr. Van Der Lann cheerfully. "Do not worry, Hanny."

"She spoke also of a customer, Mrs. Gabriel. And a large order of tulip bulbs from Holland."

The nurseryman became attentive, listening closely as his niece related the entire conversation overheard in the hayloft.

"The Mattoxes are welcome to their big order," he said. "I can tell you no more, Hanny, except to say that you are never to talk to Mrs. Gabriel or have anything to do with her."

"But why, Uncle Peter?"

"Do not ask me questions," he said kindly. "I cannot answer, Hanny. Mrs. Gabriel is not to be trusted. I have told her never to come here."

Mr. Van Der Lann would say no more about Mrs. Gabriel. As it now was growing dusk, he told Vevi he would take her home in his car.

"When you see the other Brownies, let them know that their wooden shoes will be ready for them by tomorrow night," he said as he dropped her off at her doorstep. "Also, unless it rains again, there will be tulips for the booth which is to be decorated."

Now that Mrs. Langley's flower show was close at hand, the Brownie Scouts dropped all other activities.

Miss Gordon and Miss Mohr had obtained Dutch girl costumes for the girls. A carpenter on the Langley estate helped out by making a booth for the organization to use. It was set up on the lawn not far from the greenhouse where the flowers were to be judged.

On the day before the show, the Brownies all hiked out to Windmill Farm. Their wooden shoes were ready for them, and all were a perfect fit.

Mr. Van Der Lann was too busy picking tulips

The Man in Gray

to talk to the children. He left word with his housekeeper though, that they were to have all the flowers they needed. Hanny helped the Brownies choose the blooms they wanted.

"My, I wish we had a tulip bed," Vevi remarked. "Miss Mohr, could the Brownie Scouts have a little plot of ground at the library?"

"Yes, I've been thinking about it, and I know just the place," the librarian replied. "It will be too late for spring bulbs. However, once the ground is prepared, you can set out other plants."

"I would rather have tulips," Vevi said, burying her nose in the crimson bouquet she had gathered. "They are the most beautiful flowers in the world."

"I would like a bed of nothing but Golden Beauties," declared Connie.

"How soon can we have our flower bed?" Sunny Davidson asked.

"I will have the plot spaded and raked tomorrow so that the ground is even and workable," the librarian promised. "If you speak to Mrs. Langley about it, I am sure she will give you plants from her estate."

"I'd like pansies," Rosemary said. "And forget-me-nots."

Sunny thought the bed should be planted with marigolds or late-flowering plants such as asters or chrysanthemums. Connie favored geraniums, while Jane thought an old fashioned herb garden would be the most interesting.

"I just want tulips," Vevi said again. "The Brownies should have a tulip garden while the festival is going on."

"I wish we had thought of it earlier," Miss Gordon replied. "Since we didn't, I am afraid you will have to forget the tulip bed, Vevi."

After gathering armfuls of tulips at Windmill Farm, the girls set the stems in tubs of water so they would not wilt.

Just then Mr. Van Der Lann came in from the field. He spoke to everyone and bestowed a very special smile upon Miss Mohr.

"I am driving to the Langley estate now in my truck," he said. "I will be glad to take the tubs of flowers there for you."

"May we ride too?" Jane asked.

"Yes, I have plenty of room," he assured her. "Jump in."

Mr. Van Der Lann was carrying a load of potted

plants to the estate. The children had never seen so many beautiful tulips.

"It will be fun riding with the flowers!" cried Vevi. "I want to sit beside the Golden Beauty."

The choice tulip, however, was not among the other potted plants in the back of the truck. Vevi was very worried about it until she discovered that the nurseryman was carrying his best tulips in a special box on the front seat.

At the Langley estate dozens of gardeners were hard at work preparing the grounds for the coming affair.

The grass was being cut with big power mowers. All of the hedges had been neatly trimmed. One worker was edging the walks.

Mr. Van Der Lann drove his truck close to the greenhouse. While he was lifting out his flowers, the Brownies went on ahead into the building.

"My, it's hot in here!" Vevi exclaimed. "It takes my breath away."

The Brownies spied Mrs. Langley telling workmen how to arrange different flower exhibits. Mr. Piff was there too. The girls saw him start to put up a poster advertising the Rosedale tulip festival.

"No! No! Not in here, of all places!" Mrs. Langley exclaimed. "You will ruin the artistic effect."

"Where shall I put the poster?" the promoter asked. He seemed rather annoyed by Mrs. Langley's refusal to let him tack it up in the greenhouse.

"Not anywhere on the estate, please."

"Don't you want to advertise the festival?"

"This is a private, non-commercial judging show," Mrs. Langley explained. "I can't have the grounds cluttered with cheap signs."

"Cheap signs!" Mr. Piff exploded. "Well, I like that! Let me tell you, if we don't advertise, the festival will be a flop. Your money is invested in it too."

"How well I know," replied Mrs. Langley coldly. "I deeply regret that I allowed you to talk me into the affair. Your methods—"

The garden club president did not finish what she had intended to say. At that instant she saw the tulips which Mr. Van Der Lann had brought into the greenhouse.

"Oh, such beautiful flowers!" she exclaimed. "I have never seen more lovely blooms. And this golden-hued tulip! What is it, Mr. Van Der Lann?"

The Man in Gray

"A new variety I am introducing," the nurseryman replied politely. "I call it the Golden Beauty."

"It is the showiest flower so far brought in."

"Thank you, Ma'am, for the praise," said the nurseryman. "I only wish that you were to be one of the judges."

While Mr. Van Der Lann was arranging his display, Mr. and Mrs. Mattox drove up in their truck. They too had brought many gorgeous flowers for the judging contest.

"Look at that rosy-red tulip," Connie directed Vevi's attention to a potted plant which Mrs. Mattox was showing to the garden club president. "Isn't it pretty?"

The tulip which Mrs. Mattox had named Candy Stick, resembled peppermint. It stood on a tall, graceful stem, its outer petals a cherry-rose color. Inside petals were a delicate white.

Vevi was deeply worried when she saw the handsome tulip. For a second she thought it was a prettier flower than the one Peter Van Der Lann had developed. Then she decided that the Golden Beauty was the better.

"They're both very nice," Connie said. "I hope

though, that Peter's tulip wins the blue ribbon tomorrow."

After admiring all the lovely flowers, the Brownies helped Miss Mohr and Miss Gordon decorate the outdoor booth. They put up colored crepe paper to cover the rough boards and pasted on the tulips they had made at the library. When the job finally was finished, the Brownies were very proud of their work.

"I just hope a wind doesn't come along tonight and ruin everything," Vevi said anxiously. "That would be too mean."

"Or a rain," added Connie, glancing up at the slightly overcast sky.

"If it should rain, workmen will move the booth indoors," Miss Mohr reassured the girls. "I think though, that tomorrow will be fair."

Her prediction proved true. The day of the flower show dawned warm and clear.

Vevi and Connie were up with the birds. Even before breakfast they were dressed in their Dutch costumes, ready to go to Mrs. Langley's estate.

By ten o'clock all of the Brownies, including Hanny, had arrived on the grounds. First of all, be-

The Man in Gray

fore taking turns working at the stand, the children visited the greenhouse where the tulips were to be judged.

In addition to the Golden Beauty and the Candy Stripe, other varieties had been displayed by Rosedale growers. There were groupings of Parrot tulips, Darwins and hybrids. One section of the room was devoted to tiny tulips suitable only for rock gardens.

"Do you think the Golden Beauty will win?" Hanny anxiously asked her little friends.

"Of course," said Vevi loyally.

"Uncle Peter says that Mr. and Mrs. Mattox have a very fine tulip," Hanny went on. "The judges seem to like it too."

Now two men and a lady had been selected to award the prize ribbons. The three were experts in judging tulips. They wandered back and forth between the rows of flowers, making notes on paper. Now and then they whispered together. It was hard to tell though, which tulip they thought was the best.

Vevi noticed a tall stranger in a gray suit who had entered the greenhouse. He seemed to be watching the persons who came in, rather than looking at the flowers.

"Who is that man?" Vevi asked, pointing him out to Hanny and Connie.

"No one I ever saw before," Connie replied carelessly. "Maybe he is one of Mr. Piff's friends."

The stranger, however, did not speak to the flower festival promoter when the latter came into the greenhouse. In fact, the man did not talk to anyone.

"Maybe he is a detective," Vevi decided. "Mrs. Langley may have hired him to watch the prize tulips."

Convinced that this was so, she went over to asked the garden club president about it.

"No, dear," Mrs. Langley assured her, "I do not have a detective on the grounds."

"Then who is that man who keeps watching everyone so closely?" Vevi asked.

Mrs. Langley turned to glance at the tall man in the gray suit. She had never seen him before.

"He probably is from some nearby town," she told Vevi. "Many persons are here today that I do not know."

"Maybe he is a friend of Mrs. Gabriel," Vevi speculated.

She had noticed that the man kept watching both Mrs. Gabriel and the Mattox couple who had come to the show together.

The Man in Gray

"Who is Mrs. Gabriel?" inquired Mrs. Langley absently. She was not paying very much attention to the conversation for her mind was on other important matters.

"Mrs. Gabriel is very fond of flowers," Vevi remarked. "I guess she must have one of the largest gardens in Rosedale."

"Why do you think that, dear?"

Mrs. Langley knew every interesting garden in the entire city and had never heard of one maintained by a Mrs. Gabriel.

"Because Mrs. Gabriel buys so many tulip bulbs." Vevi replied. "She tried to place a very large order with Peter Van Der Lann. When he wouldn't take it, she went to the Mattox Nursery with her business."

Mrs. Langley now was listening more attentively to the little girl. Neither of them noticed that the stranger in gray had moved closer. He too could hear their conversation.

"You say Mr. Van Der Lann turned down a very large bulb order?" the garden club president asked. "Well, that is odd. I wonder why?"

"He didn't seem to like Mrs. Gabriel."

"Mrs. Gabriel—" repeated the society woman,

mulling over the name. "I'm quite sure I never have heard of her, or her garden. Why would she order tulips at this time of year? Perhaps it was for fall delivery. No doubt that was it, Vevi. Mr. Van Der Lann turned down the business, because this isn't a good time to plant bulbs. Any that were bought now would have to be held until Fall."

Mrs. Langley was called away just then and so said no more about Mrs. Gabriel. However, the man in gray moved over to where Vevi stood.

"Hello, little girl," he greeted her. And in a friendly voice, he asked: "Which lady is Mrs. Gabriel? Is she the one in the darkblue dress?"

"Oh, no, that is Mrs. Howard," Vevi answered. "Mrs. Gabriel is over by the door, talking to Peter Van Der Lann."

"The owner of Windmill Farm?"

Vevi merely nodded and did not answer. She had begun to wonder why the man asked so many curious questions.

"Say, you must be a detective," she declared, after studying him a moment.

The man only smiled. He started to ask Vevi another question, but before he could do so, Mrs.

Langley clapped her hands to attract everyone's attention.

The room became very quiet.

"The judges are ready to award the prize ribbons," announced the garden club president. "Clear the aisles, please. In a moment now, we will know which tulip is considered the best in the show."

Chapter 12

A FLOWER SHOW

AN expectant hush fell upon the crowd as Mrs. Langley made her announcement.

Everyone watched the three judges, wondering which tulip they would choose for the first prize award.

"Oh, they're stopping beside the candy stripe tulip!" Vevi whispered nervously to Connie. "That is the flower they are going to choose."

Connie thought so too and so did Hanny who stood beside the two Brownies. Her tense face puckered up and she looked as if she were about to burst into tears.

"If Uncle Peter's tulip doesn't win, I'll have to go back to the orphanage in Holland," she whispered. "I know it!"

The judges were now pinning a ribbon on the table where the candy stripe tulip was displayed.

"The Mattox flower wins," Hanny said with a little moan. "Oh, I was afraid of it. The flower is very beautiful."

A Flower Show

"But not half as nice as the Golden Beauty," Vevi declared loyally. "I don't see how the judges could make such a mistake."

"They haven't!" cried Connie. "Just look at the color of the ribbon, you dopes!"

Hanny and Vevi laughed aloud, so great was their relief. True, the judges had pinned a ribbon on the Mattox' table. But it was not a blue ribbon. Instead, it was red and bore printing which said "Second Prize."

"The first prize hasn't been awarded yet," Hanny said, breathing naturally again. "Uncle Peter still has a chance."

Again the judges paused, this time beside the table on which stood the Golden Beauty. They whispered together. Then one of the men pinned the blue ribbon on Peter Van Der Lann's choice flower.

"He's won first prize!" shouted Vevi. "Hurrah!"

Hanny couldn't say a word. Tears streamed down her cheeks. This time, however, they were tears of happiness.

Everyone crowded about the nurseryman, offering congratulations. At once, flower lovers began asking him how they could obtain bulbs of the Golden Beauty for fall planting.

Mr. Piff pushed through the throng to shake Peter's hand.

"Congratulations!" he boomed. "Mr. Van Der Lann, you and I will have to make a deal. I understand you have a good stock of bulbs on hand. Now that you've won first prize, I can arrange to sell them for you at a fancy price. My commission will be very small—"

"You will receive no commission from me," the nurseryman broke in. He made it plain that he wanted nothing whatsoever to do with the promoter. "I have already arranged to sell my entire stock to a large seed house in the East. Now that I have won the blue ribbon, the bulbs will command a good price."

Hanny was so happy over her uncle's good fortune that she scarcely could contain her joy. She went skipping over the grounds, telling everyone about the Golden Beauty.

"Now you know why I called the locked room our treasure house!" she said to Vevi. "All those fine bulbs that are stored there will be worth their weight in gold."

"My, I wish the Brownies had a bed of Golden

A Flower Show

Beauty tulips," remarked Rosemary Fritche, who had listened to the talk.

"So do I," added Vevi wistfully.

"I will give you some of the bulbs," Hanny offered.

"Not of the Golden Beauty?" Rosemary asked in amazement.

Hanny nodded. "I will give you some of the culls," she promised. "They are bulbs that are too small to sell. Each one will bear a flower, but it will not be large."

"That wouldn't matter," Vevi said. "When may we have the bulbs?"

"Come to Windmill Farm when we leave here and I will give you a bag of them," Hanny offered.

Throughout most of the day, the Brownie Scouts remained at the Langley estate. They took turns working at the flower stand. Tussie-mussie bouquets sold very well at twenty-five cents each. The girls also disposed of many tulips.

When they sold out, Mr. Van Der Lann and Hanny drove to Windmill Farm in the truck to bring more flowers.

"My, but the Brownies have made a lot of

money," Jane Tuttle remarked, jingling the coins in the cash box. "Shall we count it?"

"Let's," agreed Vevi. "You start on the nickels and pennies. I will take the dimes and quarters."

The large coins were easy to count. Vevi reported very quickly that they amounted to ten dollars and forty cents.

Jane had to count the pennies and nickels twice. She kept getting mixed up.

"There are two dollars and a quarter in nickels," she finally decided. "I think the pennies add up to a dollar and three cents."

"That makes thirteen dollars!" exclaimed Vevi. "The Brownies are rich!"

"Thirteen dollars and sixty-eight cents," corrected Connie who was better at arithmetic than her little friend.

Miss Gordon told the children she would take charge of the money for them. Sunny Davidson asked what the organization would do with the fund.

"Will we have a nice party?" she questioned.

"We could," Miss Gordon agreed. "I wonder though, if the girls wouldn't prefer to do something really worthwhile. Miss Mohr has a suggestion."

A Flower Show

The librarian's proposal was that the Brownie Scout troop use some of its money to send a CARE package of children's books to a foreign country.

"Any country?" asked Vevi.

"Yes, the girls may make their choice."

"Italy," cried Jane before any of the other Brownies could speak. She named that particular country just to tease Vevi.

"No, Holland!" insisted Vevi. "That's where I want the package to go!"

Usually, the other Brownies had ideas that were very different from hers. This time, however, everyone except Jane agreed with her. Because of Hanny, all the troop members wanted the book package to be sent to Holland.

"I'll vote for Holland too," declared Jane, changing her vote.

"That matter is settled then," Miss Mohr said, well pleased by the decision. "I'll take care of the matter."

The Brownies had worked hard at their stand and now were tired and ready to go home. Everyone said the flower show had been a great success. Hundreds of persons had visited the estate, admiring the beautiful plantings.

Mr. Piff and the Mattox couple were the only ones who did not seem pleased.

"This flower show was a mistake," the promoter complained. "The affair has attracted so many persons that it may hurt attendance at the big festival later this week."

"The festival will be an anti-climax," agreed Mr. Mattox. "I wish you hadn't talked me into contributing so much money."

"You made us believe that our tulip would win the prize and that we would make a great deal from the sale of bulbs," Mrs. Mattox accused the promoter. "Now Peter Van Der Lann wins the blue ribbon and he had nothing to do with the festival! It is unfair!"

"Was it my fault the judges didn't choose your tulip?" Mr. Piff growled. "Let me tell you I've had my troubles! Everyone is complaining—jumping on me—saying I haven't kept my promises."

"Maybe you'd like to get out of the whole mess?" suggested Mr. Mattox.

"I sure would! I'm fed up with Rosedale and this stupid festival."

"You're fed up! You're starting to make excuses because you are afraid the thing will be a flop. Well,

A Flower Show

let me tell you this, Mr. Piff. You promised that if we put in five thousand dollars, we'd get it back in bulb sales. You'd better make good!"

"Oh, you make me tired," Mr. Piff retorted.

He walked angrily off and the Brownies did not hear any more. A little later though, they saw the president of the Rosedale Savings Bank talking soberly to the promoter.

"Mr. Piff is in trouble with everyone," Miss Gordon told the Brownies. "He has obtained heavy contributions from Rosedale businessmen and flower growers. However, he failed with his publicity, and now the businessmen are afraid they will lose nearly everything they put into the affair."

Visitors began to leave the Langley grounds. Connie's mother presently drove all the Brownies except Vevi, to their homes. Vevi, who wanted to obtain the bag of Golden Beauty culls, said she would wait until Mr. Van Der Lann and Hanny were ready to leave.

The nurseryman loaded his truck with plants and drove to Windmill Farm, taking both Hanny and Vevi with him.

"I will have to make one more trip," he told them after he had unloaded. "Then I will take you home, Vevi."

The two girls decided to wait at the farm until Mr. Van Der Lann returned. He promised he would be back within a half hour at the latest.

"Look after everything, Hanny," he instructed.

After Mr. Van Der Lann had gone with the truck, Hanny and Vevi had a snack of cheese and crackers. Then they decided to get the bag of tulip culls.

"Are you sure your uncle will not mind?" Vevi asked.

"Oh, he will want you to have them, Vevi. The bulbs are too small to be sold. He is giving Miss Mohr some Golden Beauty tulips too. Only he will let her have choice stock."

"I guess that is because he likes her better than anyone else," Vevi said with a giggle.

She knew that Mr. Van Der Lann and the pretty librarian twice had been seen together at the movies. Everyone in Rosedale, it seemed, had talked about it, saying they made a nice couple.

"It is getting late," Vevi said, deciding not to tease her little friend about Miss Mohr. "I should be starting home."

"I will fetch the bulbs," Hanny offered. "They are in the barn."

Vevi went with her to the building. While they

A Flower Show

were inside, Hanny tossed several ears of corn into the cow's manger.

After that she sorted through several bags of bulbs until she found the one for which she searched.

"When you plant these, use a little fertilizer with them," she instructed. "That will make them grow faster. And press the bulbs down firmly, so there will be no air pockets."

Vevi picked up the bag and started to leave the barn. In the open doorway she paused and uttered an exclamation of surprise.

"You have a visitor, Hanny," she said.

"A customer?" inquired Hanny. "Not the Mattox couple again!"

She went quickly to the door. Vevi pointed toward the locked house where the choice tulip bulbs were stored.

A man stood at the door, apparently tampering with the padlock. His back was toward the barn, so the children could not immediately see who he was.

As they watched, he moved slightly. Then they obtained a plain view of his face.

"Why, it is that same man in gray who attended

the flower show at Mrs. Langley's!" Vevi exclaimed. "What is he doing here? Why is he trying to break into the little house?"

Chapter 13

A BAG OF TULIPS

AS the two girls watched, the man in gray merely shook the padlock, but did not try to smash it open.

Hanny and Vevi hurried over to the little house.

"Why are you trying to break in?" Hanny demanded severely of the stranger.

"Just checking," he replied. He smiled at her in a friendly way, not acting in the least as if he had been caught trying to steal or do anything dishonest. "Is your uncle at home, Hanny?"

"No, he isn't," Hanny answered. She was astonished that the man knew her first name.

"What are you doing here anyhow?" questioned Vevi alertly. "You're not a detective, are you?"

Once a long while before, the little girl had been carried away with a circus and during the exciting trip had met a detective. The manner of this quiet stranger reminded her somewhat of the other investigator.

The Brownie Scouts at Windmill Farm

"My name is Frederick Evans," the man replied. "I'm with the FBI."

"The FBI!" gasped Vevi, deeply impressed. "Is that the secret service?"

"FBI stands for Federal Bureau of Investigation. I'm doing a little investigating."

Mr. Evans then began to ask casual questions about Hanny's uncle and the various customers who came to his farm. He inquired as to recent shipments of tulip bulbs from Holland and whether or not Mr. Van Der Lann had any helpers.

"Only me," Hanny replied to the last question. "We did have a hired man earlier this spring. But now he is working for Mr. and Mrs. Mattox."

Mr. Evans next asked if Hanny's uncle had a customer by the name of Mrs. Gabriel.

"Oh, no!" the little girl returned with emphasis. "She used to come here, but Uncle Peter told her he did not want her business."

"Did he tell you why?"

Hanny shook her head. She had been made very uneasy by so many questions about her uncle.

"I'll drop around later when Mr. Van Der Lann is at home," the FBI man said to reassure her. "He may be able to help me."

A Bag of Tulips

Very shortly the stranger left without explaining why he had come to Windmill Farm or what he was investigating. Hanny, however, was very worried.

"FBI men always arrest people, don't they?" she remarked nervously to Vevi. "Why would he come here?"

"Maybe he thinks your uncle has done something wrong."

"Not Uncle Peter," declared Hanny. "No, it is about Mrs. Gabriel, I think. Oh, dear, I wish my uncle were here. I'm worried."

By this time it was quite late. Mr. Van Der Lann had been gone much longer than half an hour. Vevi knew she would have to start home at once if she were to be on time for supper.

"I must go right away," she said. "I will see you tomorrow, Hanny. Thanks a lot for the bag of bulbs."

"Uncle Peter will take you home if you wait."

"I had better go now," Vevi decided. "My Mother will be expecting me."

Hanny walked with her to the gate. The bus did not run very often, so Vevi set off afoot.

At first the bag of tulip bulbs did not seem very heavy. But as she trudged on over the rolling hills, it seemed to take on added weight. Several times she had to stop and set it down on the pavement a moment to rest her arm.

"My I wish someone would offer me a ride," she thought wearily.

Two cars sped past. The drivers did not appear to notice the tired little girl.

Presently, another automobile rolled over a hill, coming from the direction of the Mattox Farm. Vevi glanced hopefully over her shoulder.

Noticing that the driver of the car was Mrs. Gabriel she was certain she would not be offered a ride.

She was surprised, therefore, when the big powerfully-built automobile coasted to a standstill beside her.

"Hello, little girl," said Mrs. Gabriel in a very friendly voice. "May I give you a lift to Rosedale?"

Now Vevi did not like Mrs. Gabriel. She wanted to turn down the ride, but she was dreadfully tired.

"Thank you," she accepted politely, "This bag is very heavy."

"Tulip bulbs?" asked Mrs. Gabriel, opening the car door.

"Just some culls that Hanny gave me."

A Bag of Tulips

As Vevi slid into the car, she noticed that canvas bags, very similar to the one she carried, were piled on the floor.

"I see you bought some tulip bulbs yourself," she remarked. "Or were they given to you?"

"I bought them," Mrs. Gabriel answered shortly. "They are special stock. The shipment I ordered direct from Holland came today."

"Are they nicer bulbs than Mr. Van Der Lann's Golden Beauty?"

"Mr. Van Der Lann!" replied Mrs. Gabriel. "His tulips are greatly over-rated. Even if he did win a blue ribbon, I prefer to do business with Mr. and Mrs. Mattox."

Now Vevi thought that Mrs. Gabriel could not possibly have bought bulbs that would produce flowers nicer than the Golden Beauty. However, she was too polite to say so.

She dropped her bag of culls down on the floor among the other sacks. Then, curious to see if the Mattox bulbs were larger than the culls Hanny had given her, she started to open one of Mrs. Gabriel's bags.

"Don't do that," the woman reprimanded her sharply.

"I'm sorry," Vevi apologized, drawing back her hand.

"I can't have tulip bulbs rolling around loose on the car floor," Mrs. Gabriel added.

Vevi was careful not to touch the bags after that. Nevertheless, she thought that Mrs. Gabriel was a very disagreeable woman.

For the first few minutes of the ride, the woman scarcely spoke. Then, in a much more friendly manner, she began to question Vevi about where she had been after leaving the flower show.

"Only to Hanny's place," the little girl replied.

"I saw a car at the gate when I drove by earlier this afternoon," Mrs. Gabriel remarked. "It was an automobile I never had noticed there before."

"It must have belonged to the stranger," answered Vevi carelessly.

"Stranger?"

"The same man who was at Mrs. Langley's flower show. He's here checking up on folks."

"Checking up on whom?"

Vevi shrugged and did not answer. She remembered that Hanny had said she thought the FBI man might be investigating Mrs. Gabriel. But what could the woman have done wrong?

A Bag of Tulips

Riding along so comfortably in the big, powerful car, Vevi found herself liking Mrs. Gabriel a tiny bit. The next moment, though, the feeling was gone. Mrs. Gabriel spoke very harshly.

"A Federal investigator, I'll warrant! The snoop!"

At the outskirts of Rosedale, Mrs. Gabriel pulled up at the curb.

"You will have to get out here," she said shortly. "I can't take you any farther."

Vevi was surprised for she had expected that Mrs. Gabriel would carry her at least to within a few blocks of her home. She began to suspect that the woman had picked her up only so that she might ask questions.

"Thank you for bringing me this far," Vevi nevertheless said politely. "I can walk the rest of the way. It is only six or eight blocks."

Mrs. Gabriel swung open the car door, impatiently waiting for the little girl to alight.

"Oh, my tulip bulbs!" Vevi exclaimed, nearly forgetting them.

She picked up the bag from the floor, and started to thank Mrs. Gabriel again for the ride.

Before she could do so, the woman drove rapidly away.

Vevi watched the car until it was out of sight. As far as she could see, Mrs. Gabriel did not turn off the main highway.

"She could have taken me farther, but she didn't want to," Vevi thought resentfully. "She just wanted to get rid of me."

Picking up the bag of tulip bulbs, the little girl trudged slowly on toward home. The sack seemed heavier than ever now.

Before she had gone half a block, it seemed to her that her arm would break.

Vevi paused beside a fence to rest. She noticed that the canves bag had the numerals 67543 stamped on the canvas. Also in black letters were printed the name of a city in Holland.

"That's funny," reflected Vevi. "I thought Hanny gave me an old bag without any markings on it. I guess I didn't notice very well."

Picking up the bag once more, she started on. Every few yards she had to shift it to the other hand. Even so, she began to wish she never had tried to carry the bulbs home.

"I should have waited for Mr. Van Der Lann," she thought. "I never knew culls could be so heavy."

Now the joke actually was on Vevi. Though she

A Bag of Tulips

did not suspect it, the bag of bulbs Hanny had given her was at this moment being carried away in Mrs. Gabriel's car.

Unknowingly, the little girl had picked up another bag in exchange. The mistake was certain to cause a great deal of trouble for Mrs. Gabriel, but of this, Vevi was blissfully unaware.

Chapter 14

MR. PIFF'S TROUBLES

"MOTHER, how can the Brownie Scouts have a tulip bed—one that will grow fast?"

Vevi asked the question at the breakfast table. It was the morning after Mrs. Langley's flower show and she still felt rather tired.

"A tulip bed?" repeated Vevi's mother absently. She was reading the paper and not paying too much attention to the conversation. "I am afraid it is too late for this year, dear."

"Hanny gave me a bag of bulbs yesterday, Mother."

"Why, that's fine," approved Mrs. McGuire. "You can wrap them in paper and keep them in a cool place until fall."

"But I want tulips right away," Vevi insisted. "How can I make them grow fast?"

"I'm afraid you can't, dear. Nurserymen sometimes 'force' plants to bring them to flower earlier or out of season. That however, takes special skill and exact temperatures. Fertilizer, of course, helps to make plants develop fast."

"I'd like to force my bulbs," Vevi announced. "The Brownies have such a nice bed at the library now. But so far it is only bare ground."

"It is too late to plant tulip bulbs this spring," said Mrs. McGuire. "The Brownies, I am afraid, will have to be satisfied with late flowering plants."

The information disappointed Vevi. After seeing so many beautiful tulips at Windmill Farm, she felt she never would be happy to have the Brownie bed devoted to any other flower. Besides, she was eager to discover if the Golden Beauty culls really would bloom.

"Today is the first day of the flower festival," Mrs. McGuire remarked. "From all I hear, the affair will not be a success."

"I think I will take a book to the library," Vevi announced. She knew it would give her an excuse to go down town to see what was happening.

"Don't stay long, dear," Mrs. McGuire advised.

Vevi felt very light hearted as she tripped along the street. Colored bunting decorated the lamp posts and hung from overhead wires on Main Street.

As Vevi reached the library, a parade went by.

Hearing the band music, she paused to watch. The beat and rumble of the drum made her blood race.

Not many people were watching the parade, and it did not last long. There were a few floats and several automobiles carrying flags. Almost before Vevi knew it, the procession had ended.

"I don't call that much of a parade," said a voice directly behind Vevi.

She whirled around to see Connie and Jane standing behind her. It was Jane who had spoken. Both girls wore their Brownie uniforms.

"My, you startled me!" Vevi laughed. "What brought you girls downtown?"

"The flower festival," explained Connie. "Only so far it doesn't amount to anything."

"Hardly anyone is attending," declared Jane. "My father says Mr. Piff has made a mess of the show. Everyone is dissatisfied."

The girls went into the library with Vevi who returned her books. They stopped to chat with Miss Mohr a moment, noticing a bouquet of beautiful scarlet tulips on her desk.

"I can guess where those came from!" laughed Connie. "Windmill Farm!"

"That is right," agreed the librarian. "Peter

Mr. Piff's Trouble

brought them over himself early this morning."

The Brownie Scouts noticed that Miss Mohr used the name "Peter" instead of Mr. Van Der Lann. Jane winked at Vevi who understand what she meant. By this time all the Brownies knew that Miss Mohr and Mr. Van Der Lann were the best of friends. In fact, the couple had been seen together at several social gatherings.

"Oh, by the way, girls," said Miss Mohr "The Brownie garden has been spaded and raked. It is ready now for the planting of seeds."

"Tulips?" inquired Vevi hopefully. "Hanny gave me a bagful of bulbs. I have them at home."

"Tulips would be nice," replied Miss Mohr. She was busy checking out a book and spoke absently. "When the right time comes to plant—"

"Most of the bulbs in my bag are Golden Beauties," Vevi told Jane and Connie. "When they bloom, they will be the best tulips in Rosedale!"

Miss Mohr had finished waiting on another child who had asked for a special book on frogs. Returning to the Brownies she reported that she had a special message for Vevi.

"Mrs. Gabriel is looking for you," the librarian said. "She came here not an hour ago, asking where you lived. She said it was most important that she find you right away."

The message astonished Vevi. She could not guess why Mrs. Gabriel would want to see her.

"Where does Mrs. Gabriel live?" she asked the librarian. "I could go to her house if it is important."

Miss Mohr said she did not have the woman's address. "It's odd," she added, "but no one in Rosedale seems to know where she lives, or for that matter, very much about her."

"Why does she want to see me, Miss Mohr?"

"She didn't say, Vevi. However, she seemed very disturbed about something."

"You've been in mischief again, I'll bet!" teased Jane, pointing an accusing finger at Vevi.

"I have not! She gave me a ride part way home from Windmill Farm yesterday. I was nice as pie to her."

Vevi was a little worried to know that Mrs. Gabriel was looking for her. She could not think of anything she had done or said that would cause the woman to seek her.

Leaving the library, the three girls went out to look at the flower bed.

Mr. Piff's Trouble

The plot was circular, nicely rounded in the center. It had been deeply spaded and the soil raked until it was nearly as fine as sand grains.

"I'll bet my tulips would grow fast here!" Vevi said. "If I plant them right away, maybe they will bloom by summer."

"Dope!" chided Jane. "Tulips only bloom in the Spring."

"Maybe it depends on when you plant them," Vevi argued. "Folks plant bulbs in the fall for Spring blooms. So if you plant in the Spring, why wouldn't the flowers come in summer?"

"And if you plant in the summer, I suppose the tulips would bloom in the winter!" Connie joked. "Oh, Vevi!"

"You heard Miss Mohr say I could plant tulips."

"She did, that's true," Connie admitted.

"Those Golden Beauty culls Hanny gave me are something special, don't forget," Vevi argued. "Miss Mohr must know all about them. That's probably why she said I could plant them now. Their growing season must be shorter than for other tulips."

"She wasn't paying much attention to what you said," Jane recalled doubtfully. "I don't think she really heard—"

The Brownie Scouts at Windmill Farm

"Oh, yes, she did," Vevi cut in. "Miss Mohr said I could plant tulips, and she meant it too."

"I think pansies would be nicer," Jane argued. "I saw a pretty basket of them a few minutes ago on my way to the library."

"No pansies," Vevi said emphatically. "That would cost money. I have the tulip bulbs and they didn't cost a penny."

Jane and Connie reluctantly abandoned the argument. Having won her point, Vevi now was eager to plant the bulbs immediately.

"You'll need tools," Jane pointed out. "Do you have a trowel?"

"What's that?"

"Oh, a thing you dig with. We have one at home. Then you ought to have fertilizer to put with each bulb. I know because I've watched my father plant things lots of times."

"Let's go to your house and get the stuff we'll need," proposed Vevi.

Jane protested that she had come down town to see the flower festival. She was not ready as yet to return home.

"Let's look at the flowers quick then," Vevi urged. "Most of the exhibits are at the auditorium."

Mr. Piff's Trouble

The girls walked to the centrally located public building. At the door they discovered that tickets were required in order to get inside.

"I don't have fifty cents," Vevi announced. "Even if I did I wouldn't spend it to see flowers growing in pots. I would rather look at them free on Windmill Farm."

"Anyway, hardly anyone is in the auditorium," Connie observed, peering through the open door.

The girls caught a glimpse of a room filled with all types of spring flowers. In the center of the hall, an artificial fountain splashed into a shallow tank where goldfish swam.

"That fountain isn't nearly as nice as the one on Mrs. Langley's estate," Jane said.

"There aren't many flowers either," added Connie. "See all the blank spaces along the wall where there should be exhibits."

As the three were peering in, Mr. Piff came along.

"Children you are blocking the door," he scolded. "Stand aside so that folks can get into the auditorium."

"There aren't any folks trying to get in," Jane replied. "I guess you aren't selling many tickets."

Mr. Piff scowled, not liking the little girl's observation. Then he smiled wryly and admitted that she was right.

"Do you girls want to go inside?" he inquired. "Pass right on in."

"Free?" Vevi asked quickly.

"Go ahead," Mr. Piff directed. "What's the difference? This show is a flop and everyone knows it."

"Maybe more people will come tomorrow," Connie said kindly.

"Tomorrow will be worse than today," Mr. Piff rejoined. "I only hope I won't be here to hear the squawks of the business men when they find out how deep in the hole we're going to be."

"You're not going away?" Connie asked quickly.

"No, no, certainly not." Mr. Piff laughed, but in a hollow sort of way.

Following the girls into the auditorium, he voiced a steady stream of complaints.

"This show would have been a success if it hadn't been for Peter Van Der Lann. That stubborn Dutchman hung the sign on me by refusing to cooperate. Then some of the other growers wouldn't come into the scheme. Mrs. Langley put in some money, quite a nice chunk, but a few days ago, she clamped down the lid. Wouldn't give me another penny.

Mr. Piff's Trouble

What was worse, her garden show drew all the customers away from this one."

The Brownies listened to Mr. Piff without saying much in return. They went over to the fountain to watch the goldfish swim in the basin.

"Some of the fish are dead," Vevi said, noticing the ones that floated on top of the water.

"Your flowers are wilting too," declared Jane. "It is too warm for them in here."

As the girls wandered about, looking at the potted tulips, lilies and other flowers, Mr. Piff talked to workmen. Connie heard the men ask him about their pay.

"Don't worry, you'll get it when the show ends," he told them. "Not before."

Refrigerators, stoves and dish washers were being demonstrated in the hall. The Brownies thought that having such items on sale ruined the garden effect.

After awhile, as they were watching a television set, Mr. Piff rejoined the girls.

"As I was saying," he remarked, "this show would have been a success if it hadn't been for Peter Van Der Lann. That tightwad didn't put a cent into the affair, and he's profited more than any grower in Rosedale."

"You mean because his tulip won the blue ribbon?" Vevi questioned. She did not like the way Mr. Piff was talking about Hanny's uncle.

"Sure," the promoter replied. "He won the ribbon, and now folks don't want to buy any of the bulbs on sale here. They only want stock from Van Der Lann. He'll make a fortune—that is, if he has any bulbs to sell."

"Oh, he has!" cried Vevi. "Hanny showed them to me. He has a little room with a padlock on the door. All his Golden Beauty bulbs are kept there."

"Oh, yes, I noticed that little house when I was out at Windmill Farm," Mr. Piff said thoughtfully. "So that's where he keeps his choice bulbs? I know a grower who would pay plenty to get them. Mr. Van Der Lann, though, won't do business with me."

The promoter asked the girls a few more questions about Mr. Van Der Lann's bulbs. Then, as he started to turn away, he said to Vevi:

"By the way, did Mrs. Gabriel see you?"

"Not today," answered Vevi. "I have been looking for her too."

"She was here not an hour ago. For that matter, she came especially to find you."

Vevi asked Mr. Piff if he knew why the woman wanted to see her.

"I've no idea," the promoter replied. "She was very angry though. Her exact words were these: 'That little imp had better return my property at once, or there will be trouble!'"

Chapter 15

THE BROWNIE GARDEN

VEVI'S first thought was that Mr. Piff was joking about Mrs. Gabriel.

"She didn't really say that about me!" the little girl protested.

"Oh, yes, she did," Mr. Piff corrected.

"But I don't have any of her property."

"Then you should see her and tell her so," the promoter declared. "If you don't, she may turn you over to the police."

"She couldn't do that," Vevi gasped. "She must have me mixed up with some other person."

The Brownies now had lost all interest in the flower show. Vevi wanted to find Mrs. Gabriel at once to try to clear up the misunderstanding.

From one booth to another the girls went, asking if anyone had seen Mrs. Gabriel. Finally they learned that she had left the building more than a half hour earlier. It seemed useless to try to seek her further.

The Brownie Garden

"I am not going to worry about her," Vevi decided. "I will let her find me. I am going home to get my tulip bulbs. Let's plant them right away."

"Why not wait until the next Brownie Scout meeting?" proposed Connie. "Then all the girls can help."

Vevi opposed any delay. "No, we must plant them right away," she insisted. "Every day counts if they are to bloom this summer."

Leaving the auditorium, the girls started for Jane's home to collect digging tools and fertilizer.

They were only three blocks from the Tuttle home when they spied a group of children coming toward them.

"What are they carrying?" Connie speculated.

Each child in the group of six held a double handful of plump, round objects.

"Onions," declared Jane.

"Tulip bulbs," corrected Vevi. By this time the children were quite close.

The youngsters would have dashed on past with their plunder, had not Jane stopped them.

"Say, where'd you get those?" she demanded.

The children halted, proudly showing the bulbs.

"We found 'em," one of the older boys said.

"Why, those look just like the Golden Beauty culls that Hanny gave me," Vevi commented as she gazed at the fistful of bulbs.

"I've got some bigger ones," announced another child in the group. He opened his hands to show the girls several large, plump bulbs.

"They do look like onions," declared Connie. "In Holland when times were hard, the people ate bulbs for food. Miss Mohr told me so."

Vevi thought that the bulbs, except for a few, looked like extremely good ones.

"Where did you find them?" she asked.

One of the boys indicated the direction from which he and the others had come. "Down the street a ways," he said. "They were lying in a culvert."

"Thrown away?" Vevi asked in amazement.

"Sure. Someone dumped a lot of 'em there."

"Are there any more?" Jane asked eagerly.

"Scads of 'em."

"Let's get some," Jane proposed to her friends. "Come on, before they're all gone."

Forgetting their plan to plant Vevi's tulips, the three girls raced down the street.

A block away, at the street corner, they saw the

The Brownie Garden

open culvert. Just as the boys had said, there lay hundreds of tulips, dumped on the street.

"Well, did you ever!" exclaimed Jane, amazed by the sight. "Who would throw away valuable tulips?"

"And so many of them!" gasped Connie. "Tulip bulbs are expensive. Why, there must be twenty or thirty dollars worth here at least!"

"Let's pick them all up," proposed Jane excitedly. "The ones we don't want for our own gardens, we can sell!"

A few of the bulbs had broken open or had been crushed. Many were in perfect condition. The girls filled their skirts, not stopping until they had gathered every bulb.

"We can take them to my house," Jane said. "My, but we have a lot of 'em. Enough for a wonderful garden."

Vevi noticed a piece of canvas lying in the gutter.

Putting down her skirtful of bulbs for a moment, she picked it up.

"Why, this is a bag," she said in astonishment. "It must have held some of the tulips."

"Someone dumped them here," Jane agreed. "I can't understand why, either. They look like perfectly good bulbs to me."

The Brownie Scouts at Windmill Farm

Vevi examined the canvas bag carefully. She noticed that it bore numbers and was stamped "Holland."

"That means these are imported bulbs," she declared. "This empty bag looks just like the one I have at home. The number is different though."

"You don't think Hanny or her uncle dumped these tulips here?" Connie asked.

"I'm sure they didn't," Vevi replied. "Maybe it was Mrs. Gabriel."

"Why should she do such a thing?" demanded Jane.

"It seems silly," Vevi agreed soberly. "All the same, this bag looks like some she had in her car. She told me her big Holland order had just been delivered."

"It couldn't have been Mrs. Gabriel," Jane argued. "If she had just bought the bulbs, she certainly wouldn't throw them away."

"Maybe they weren't good enough for her garden," Vevi speculated. "She's real fussy, I guess."

The girls stuffed as many bulbs as they could into the empty bag. The remainder they carried in their hands to Jane's home.

"What will we do with so many tulips?" Connie

The Brownie Garden

asked. "Shall we use them for the Brownie Scout garden at the library?"

"Oh, no," Vevi said in quick protest. "I want to plant my Golden Beauties there."

"But those bulbs are only culls," Jane argued. "Most of these are nice big fat ones."

"Maybe size doesn't count," Vevi replied. "They couldn't have been much good, or they wouldn't have been thrown away."

"That's so," agreed Connie, siding with her friend. "Maybe the bulbs are dead and won't grow. Besides, Hanny might not like it if we don't use her bulbs."

"Okay," Jane consented. "I'll get the digging tools. We can leave these bulbs in our garage until we decide where to plant them."

An empty shelf along one side of the garage provided a place for the bulbs. The girls lined them up in neat rows.

"They do look just like onions!" Jane laughed. "I hope Mother doesn't use them for a stew."

"All of the bulbs are the same size, large and plump," Connie noticed. "That is, all but about twenty or so. Vevi, you don't suppose—"

She was intending to ask Vevi if by any chance

The Brownie Scouts at Windmill Farm

she might have mixed up one of the bags with Hanny's culls. Before she could do so, however, Jane interrupted:

"If we're going to plant tulips, let's get at it!" she urged. "It's nearly lunch time now."

Jane asked permission of her mother to go to Vevi's house. Carrying the digging tools, the girls reached the McGuire home exactly at noon.

Mrs. McGuire was preparing lunch as the three Brownies stomped into the kitchen.

"Oh, here you are, Vevi," her mother said. "I've telephoned everywhere, trying to find you."

"For lunch?" the little girl asked. "I'm terribly hungry. And so are Connie and Jane. Please, may they stay?"

"Of course," agreed Mrs. McGuire. "But it wasn't because of lunch that I called you. While you were gone we had a visitor."

"Not the minister?" asked Vevi.

"No, dear, it was a woman named Mrs. Gabriel."

Hearing the name again, Vevi had a queer feeling in the pit of her stomach. She couldn't imagine what she had done wrong. It must have been something very dreadful, though, or the woman wouldn't keep trying to find her.

The Brownie Garden

"What did she want, Mother?" Vevi asked in a faint voice.

"She said you had taken something from her car. A bag of valuable tulip bulbs."

Chapter 16

MRS. GABRIEL'S ACCUSATION

VEVI became very indignant when she heard the purpose of Mrs. Gabriel's call.

"Why, how could she accuse me of such a thing?" she asked, deeply hurt. "I never took anything in my life."

"I told Mrs. Gabriel that," declared Mrs. McGuire. "She was quite demanding and rude. You did ride in her car, Vevi?"

"Yes, Mother. She offered me a lift from Windmill Farm. I think she asked me a million questions. Then she made me get out and walk part of the way."

"You didn't take anything from her car?"

"Of course not. Only the bag of tulip bulbs Hanny gave me."

"Could you have mixed the bags?"

"I don't think I did," Vevi said. "I will show you the bulbs."

For safe keeping, the little girl had stored the

Mrs. Gabriel's Accusation

bag in the basement. Quickly she brought it upstairs.

Mrs. McGuire untied the strings and peered into the bag.

"Tulip bulbs all look alike to me," she said. "If you are sure these are yours, Vevi—"

"Oh, I am, Mother!"

"Then forget Mrs. Gabriel," advised Mrs. McGuire. "To tell you the truth, her accusation annoyed me. I offered to pay her for any bulbs she thought she had lost, but that did not satisfy her. Nor would she give me her address so that I could call her after talking to you, Vevi. I am afraid she is a trouble maker."

No more was said about the bulbs. Jane and Connie stayed for lunch. After the dishes had been done, Mrs. McGuire went next door to talk with Connie's mother.

"If we are going to plant tulips we will have to do it right away," Jane announced. "It is nearly time for me to go home now."

"Maybe we shouldn't plant the Golden Beauties now," Connie suggested doubtfully. "Mrs. Gabriel might make trouble if she thinks they are her tulips."

"They're mine," Vevi said. "Hanny gave them to me. Anyway, Mrs. Gabriel didn't think so much of her precious old tulips or she wouldn't have dumped them along the roadside."

"Do you really think she did?" Connie asked.

"That empty bag looked exactly like one I saw in her car."

"But your bag—the one Hanny gave you—has the same kind of markings," Connie pointed out. "Vevi, maybe you did make a mistake and pick up the wrong one."

"No such thing," Vevi insisted emphatically. "Anyway, even if I did, Mrs. Gabriel got another bag of tulips better than her own. Everyone knows the Golden Beauties are the very best."

"That's so," agreed Jane. "Even if there was a mix-up, she came out with good tulips. I don't see why she's making such a fuss."

"Let's plant the Brownie flower bed," urged Connie who had wearied of the discussion. "Come on."

Carrying the bag of bulbs and Jane's garden tools, the girls set off for the library.

"We ought to tell Miss Mohr what we are doing," Connie suggested. "Maybe she will tell us how to do it right."

Mrs. Gabriel's Accusation

"Oh, anyone can plant tulip bulbs," Vevi said carelessly. "Hanny told me how."

Nevertheless, the three girls went into the building to find Miss Mohr. Another librarian told them that she had left twenty minutes earlier with Peter Van Der Lann.

"We don't need anyone to tell us how to plant," Vevi insisted. "It's easy."

"I guess it will be all right," Connie agreed with a troubled frown. "Only the Brownies may not like it. They may want other flowers in the bed."

"Tulips are the very best," Vevi declared. "And Golden Beauties are the nicest bulbs."

"The only thing—you aren't sure you're planting Golden Beauties," Jane teased. "For all you know, they may be Mrs. Gabriel's tulips!"

"No such thing," Vevi insisted, opening the bag. "These are my culls."

"What's a cull?" Jane asked for she was unfamiliar with the word.

"That means a bulb that isn't as good as the regular stock," Vevi explained. "It will bloom though. Hanny said so."

The little girl poured some of the bulbs out on the grass. All were well-shaped, fat specimens.

"Those look like good bulbs to me," declared Jane. "Connie, don't they seem exactly like the ones we found on the road?"

"They look the same to me."

Vevi said nothing. She began to dig a neat hole in the well-pulverized ground.

"Tulip bulbs have to be put in deep," directed Connie. "I know that, because I heard Mr. Van Der Lann telling Miss Gordon."

"I am digging the hole deep," Vevi replied. "At least six inches. That ought to be deep enough."

She pressed the first bulb down into the spot she had prepared for it.

"Hey, I thought you said you knew how to plant bulbs!" Jane hooted. "You're putting it in upside down!"

"The sprout end has to be up and the roots underneath," added Connie. "Anyone knows that, Vevi."

"Oh, I wasn't ready to plant the bulb," Vevi said, hastily turning it over. "I was only trying it in the hole to see if I had dug it the right size."

"Let me dig," Jane demanded, after the first bulb had been planted and covered with soil. "It takes you too long, Vevi."

Mrs. Gabriel's Accusation

"I'll hand you the bulbs," Vevi offered, willing enough to turn the harder job over to her friend.

Jane dug a series of small holes all around the circular bed. She worked fast and spaced them evenly.

"Now hand me the bulbs one at a time," she instructed.

Vevi dumped them all out of the bag. From the very bottom of the canvas sack out tumbled a handful of small gray, greasy appearing pellets.

"What are those?" Connie demanded curiously.

Picking up one of the hard, round pieces, she rubbed it between her fingers.

"It must be fertilizer," Vevi declared. "Put one in with each tulip bulb."

Jane followed instructions, carefully pressing a pellet at the base of each bulb. There were not enough of them to finish the task. The last of the bulbs had to be planted without the "fertilizer."

"There! That's done," Jane said in relief when the last bulb had been firmly covered with earth. "I'm tired too! My legs feel as if they will drop off."

"Your neck is all red," Connie informed her. "I think you are sunburned."

The Brownie Scouts at Windmill Farm

Jane gingerly rubbed her neck which smarted and felt uncomfortable.

"I hurt all over," she complained. "Tulips are too much work."

"I don't think they are," declared Vevi, who had dug only one hole. "Anyway, it is worth while. The Brownies will have one of the nicest flower beds in Rosedale."

"I just hope the other Brownies 'preciate all the work we've done," Jane muttered. "It's late and I'm going home."

She began to gather up the tools. Her Brownie uniform was smudged with dirt and so were her sox.

Vevi and Connie walked along with Jane, helping her carry the tools. Vevi had picked up the empty canvas bag too, not wanting to leave it on the library lawn.

Before the girls had walked three blocks, Jane noticed someone coming toward them.

"See who is heading our way!" she directed the attention of her companions.

A woman was coming down the street. As she saw the three girls, she began to walk faster.

Mrs. Gabriel's Accusation

"It's Mrs. Gabriel, Vevi recognized her. "She looks cross too."

Mrs. Gabriel's high heels were clicking like knitting needles by the time she came face to face with the trio.

"Well!" she exclaimed, glaring at Vevi. "At last I've found you!"

"I haven't been anywhere," Vevi answered innocently.

"I want my bag of tulip bulbs" Mrs. Gabriel announced.

"*Your* bag," said Vevi. "Do you mean my sack of culls that Hanny gave me?"

"Don't try to pretend. When you rode in my car, you were carrying a bag of bulbs. Either by accident, or on purpose, you left yours behind and took one of mine. I want it back—now."

"I took a bag of tulip bulbs. But I thought it was mine—"

"You're carrying the empty sack now," Mrs. Gabriel fairly screamed. "Give it to me."

She snatched the bag from Vevi's hand, excitedly examining the numerals.

"This is the sack!" she cried. "Now where are the contents?"

"I didn't mean to mix up the bags," Vevi apologized. "I thought—"

"Never mind what you thought," Mrs. Gabriel broke in angrily. "Just tell me what you did with the tulip bulbs."

"I don't see why you're so excited about it," Jane said before Vevi could answer. "You threw all your other bulbs away."

"In a culvert," added Connie accusingly.

"Why, you insolent, stupid children!" Mrs. Gabriel cried. "Such arrogance! I want my tulip bulbs. Do you understand?"

The Brownies never had seen anyone more angry. Mrs. Gabriel seized Vevi by the arm, squeezing it so hard that the muscle hurt.

"What have you done with my bulbs?" she demanded.

"Let me go and I'll tell you," Vevi answered, trying to pull away. "I never will when you act so cross."

Mrs. Gabriel dropped her arm. She even forced a stiff sort of smile.

"There, child, I didn't mean to frighten you," she said in a wheedling tone. "Just tell me what you did with the contents of the bag."

Mrs. Gabriel's Accusation

"We planted the bulbs in the Brownie Scout bed at the library," Vevi answered. "I didn't mean to take your bulbs. But you got mine. So wasn't it a fair exchange?"

"A fair exchange?" Mrs. Gabriel cried, her voice shrill. "You planted the tulips! That bag was worth a small fortune to me. Oh, I could shake you!"

Vevi backed away, rather afraid of the irate woman.

"What did you do with the pellets that were in the bag?" she demanded.

"You mean those little pieces of fertilizer?" Vevi stammered. "We planted them with the bulbs!"

"Oh!" gasped Mrs. Gabriel. She started to scold Vevi and then abandoned the tirade. With a gesture of both anger and despair, she brushed past the girls and went rapidly away.

Chapter 17

A LIBRARY WINDOW

VEVI, Connie and Jane watched Mrs. Gabriel until she was out of sight far down the street.

"Such a fuss about a few stupid tulip bulbs," Vevi said. "What's the matter with her anyhow?"

"She's an old fussbudget," Jane returned. "Why did that one bag of bulbs mean so much to her?"

"She spoke especially of the pellets that were with the bulbs," Connie said reflectively. "Whoever heard of setting such store by fertilizer?"

"Anyway, the bulbs are planted now," Vevi said with a nervous giggle. "Do you suppose she'll try to make me pay for 'em?"

"She might," Connie returned. "Mrs. Gabriel said the bulbs were worth a small fortune."

"That's silly," Vevi declared. "Even the best tulip bulbs shouldn't cost more than a dollar or two a dozen."

"Some do, I think," Connie said. "We must have planted at least four dozen."

A Library Window

"That would amount to eight or ten dollars at least," Jane computed. "Vevi, if she decides to make trouble, you're really in for it."

"Pooh! I'm not worried."

However, Vevi was only trying to put up a good front. Actually she was deeply concerned. She knew Mrs. Gabriel might accuse her of taking the tulip bulbs on purpose.

The exchange had been accidental, but one that the woman couldn't seem to understand. Vevi had less than five dollars in her savings bank at home. How could she ever pay the sum Mrs. Gabriel might ask? It made her fairly ill to think of it.

At the next corner, the girls parted to go to their separate homes. As Vevi started away alone, Connie reminded her that all the Brownie Scouts had been invited to take part in a puppet show that evening in the public library.

"Don't forget, Vevi."

"I'll be there," Vevi promised. With a nervous giggle, she added: "That is, unless Mrs. Gabriel puts me in jail!"

Miss Mohr and Miss Gordon had planned the puppet show as a special treat for the girls. The Brownies themselves had made scenery and painted

The Brownie Scouts at Windmill Farm

the clever figures which were to be used in a dramatization of "The Brownie Story" by Juliana H. Ewing.

Using patterns provided by Miss Mohr, the girls had traced them on stiff cardboard. These they had cut out, pasted and painted. Each character had a narrow, stiff strip of cardboard at the back which could be used as a handle to make the figures move in a life-like manner on the little stage.

Besides tiny elves, the girls had created a Tailor, his aging mother, Mary and her little brother, and an Old Owl.

Vevi was assigned to speak the words of the Old Owl and to handle that particular puppet.

Her part had not been hard to learn. Mostly the owl only had to say "Who-oo," and "Hoot! Hoot!"

"Don't be late," Connie warned as she and Jane bade their friend goodbye. "After the puppet show we're to have an investiture ceremony. Hanny's to be made a real Brownie."

"I'll be on time," Vevi promised again. "Hoot! Hoot!"

By seven o'clock that night all the troop members were at the library. Vevi as usual was the last to arrive. She seemed so fidgety and nervous that

A Library Window

Connie asked her if Mrs. Gabriel had made any more trouble.

"What makes you think she will?" Vevi asked quickly.

"I saw her walking around the library when I came in a few minutes ago," Connie revealed. "She was looking at the Brownie flower bed too."

"I wish you wouldn't keep talking about Mrs. Gabriel and her silly tulip bulbs," Vevi said, squirming uncomfortably. "I'm not worrying about her."

"Then what is wrong with you?"

"I'm thinking about my part in the play, that's all. I'm afraid I may forget my lines."

"Your lines!" Connie laughed. "All you have to do is hold your owl up in a tree and make bird noises. And you're afraid you'll forget!"

The girls were using a large library table for a stage. In the first scene, the Tailor and his elderly wife sat by their fireside discussing Mary and Tommy, who never liked to help with work in the home.

Connie took the part of the Old Tailor, while Rosemary spoke the lines of the aged grandmother. Sunny acted the character of Mary, and Hanny that of the little boy, Tommy.

The play progressed. In the second scene, Tommy and Mary, eager to find Brownies who would do all the housework for their family, set off to the woods to seek advice of the wise old Owl.

Vevi, thoroughly enjoying her role of owl, hooted and whoo'd and advised the children that they could find the "Brownies" only by going to the north side of the pond when the moon was shining.

"Say these words," she directed in her most owlish voice: " 'Twist me, and turn me and show me the Elf; I looked into the water, and saw—'

"Then," she further instructed, "at the moment you gaze into the water, think of a word that will rhyme with Elf, and complete the verse."

In the next scene of the playlet, Sunny and Hanny as Tommy and Mary, were shown at the pond. Gazing down into a circular mirror which represented the water, they saw their own reflections. Sunny recited:

" 'Twist me, and turn me and show me
    the Elf;
I looked into the water, and saw—' "

"Myself," Hanny completed the rhyme.

According to the story, the children then knew that they were the real Brownies. The next and final scene showed them doing cheerfully the work of the family. The playlet ended with Connie as the old grandmother, declaring that children were a blessing, not a burden.

Everyone said the show had been a great success.

"I didn't forget my lines either," Vevi laughed in relief. "Not a single hoot!"

The time now had come for Hanny formally to be invested as a Brownie Scout. She was sent from the room while the other girls gathered in a circle about the big library table.

At the proper moment, Miss Gordon told Hanny she might return.

In the story room, the lights had been switched off. For a minute Hanny was bewildered as she came in.

Then Vevi took her hand and led her to the big table. The circular mirror, which represented a pool of water, had been placed in the very center.

"Who comes to the fairy wood?" asked Miss Gordon. "I do," answered the little girl. "Hanny."

"What do you seek?"

"To be a Brownie Scout," replied Hanny earnestly.

"Why, Hanny?" asked Miss Gordon. "Why do you wish to become a Brownie?"

Hanny drew a deep breath. For a second, she couldn't think of anything to say. Then the words came with a rush.

"I want to be a Brownie because I love America!" she cried, her eyes shining. "I want to live here always. I like Rosedale too and all the girls."

"That is reason enough for becoming a Brownie," declared Miss Gordon warmly. "Now gaze into the pool."

Hanny looked down into the mirror. Miss Gordon turned her around twice, and placed a Brownie cap on her head.

" 'Twist me, and turn me, and show me the Elf;' " recited the other Brownies in unison.

" 'I looked into the pool and saw—' "

"MYSELF," cried Hanny.

The ceremony was completed by having the little girl repeat the Brownie Promise. She gave it word perfect.

Miss Gordon then pinned a Brownie Scout pin on the right-hand side of her collar. She saluted Hanny and shook her hand, using the special grasp known only to troop members.

"Am I a real Brownie now?" Hanny asked happily.

"As real as they come," declared Miss Mohr, giving her an affectionate hug.

"The best part of all is that I am going to stay in Rosedale," Hanny told the other girls. "Now that my uncle has won the blue ribbon, he will make a great deal of money. Already he has had many fine offers for the Golden Beauty tulip bulbs."

All the girls were delighted that Hanny would be able to remain in Rosedale, and told her so.

By this time it was five minutes after eight o'clock.

"Time for the meeting to end," said Miss Gordon noticing the clock. "School tomorrow as usual, you know. Little Brownies should be in bed early."

The girls began to put on their jackets and coats. Vevi had left hers in another room. She went for it but did not immediately return.

Impatiently, the other Brownies waited.

"That Vevi!" Jane exclaimed. "She always keeps us waiting!"

"What do you suppose she's doing now?" Sunny speculated.

The room where Vevi had left her jacket was dark. What, the Brownies wondered, could she be doing so long without a light?

"Hurry up Vevi!" Jane called.

There was no answer from the darkened cloak room.

"She's holding us up on purpose!" Jane fumed. "Let's leave without her. It would serve her right for being such a slow poke."

Miss Gordon, however, would not allow the Brownies to depart without Vevi.

"I'll see what is keeping her," she offered.

However, before the Brownie Scout leader could enter the darkened room, Vevi appeared in the doorway.

"Why, you don't have your jacket even now!" Jane exclaimed. "Vevi McGuire! You're the limit!"

"We've waited an age," added Rosemary.

Vevi had a strange expression on her face.

"What's wrong?" Connie asked her quickly. "Have you lost something? Your pocketbook?"

Vevi shook her head. "I want to show you something—"

"Oh, Vevi, we're in a hurry!" Jane exclaimed indignantly. "You're always holding us up."

"This is important. Someone is digging in the Brownie tulip bed."

A Library Window

"WHAT?" cried the Brownies almost as one person.

"Come and see for yourselves," invited Vevi. "You can watch from the window. All the tulip bulbs are being scattered on the ground!"

Chapter 18

MAGIC WAYS

NOW Miss Mohr and Miss Gordon had not known that tulip bulbs were planted in the Brownie Scout flower bed. Vevi, Connie and Jane had been so busy with the show that they had neglected to mention the planting.

Therefore, everyone was surprised to hear that the bulbs were being dug up.

"What do you mean?" demanded Jane in great excitement. "Who is wrecking our flower bed?"

"A woman," Vevi informed the group. "I can't see her too plainly from the window. Come quick!"

The Brownie Scouts needed no further urging. With the librarian and their leader, they followed Vevi into the darkened room overlooking the lawn.

"See, down there!" the little girl declared, pointing out the window.

The Brownies jostled each other in their eagerness to learn what was going on in the yard.

A shadowy figure could be seen on hands and knees, industriously digging up the tulip bulbs.

Magic Ways

Already many of them were scattered helter-skelter over the grass.

"Well, of all the nerve!" cried Vevi indignantly.

"It looks like Mrs. Gabriel," declared Connie. "At least she has a tall feather on her hat, just like one Mrs. Gabriel has."

"Let's stop her!" exclaimed Vevi, starting for the door.

Miss Gordon grasped her hand, holding her back "Wait, Vevi."

"Wait? But Miss Gordon, our tulip bed is nearly ruined now! She's wrecking everything!"

"And we worked so hard planting those bulbs," Jane wailed. "It's the meanest trick yet."

Miss Gordon spoke quietly.

"Mrs. Gabriel, I think, is after something more vital than tulip bulbs."

"I think so too," agreed Miss Mohr quickly. "Peter has told me of his suspicions that a ring may be operating—"

Now the Brownies were quite bewildered by the talk, not understanding what the two young women meant.

"Must we let that dreadful Mrs. Gabriel ruin our flower bed?" demanded Jane.

"No, indeed," replied Miss Mohr. "I intend to call Peter Van Der Lann and the police."

"The police?" gasped Vevi. She had not thought of having Mrs. Gabriel arrested.

"We must hurry," urged Miss Gordon, peering out the window again.

While the teacher and the Brownie Scouts kept watch, Miss Mohr telephoned the police station. Then she called Hanny's uncle at Windmill Farm.

"Peter is coming as quickly as he can drive here!" the librarian told the group tensely. "He says we must hold Mrs. Gabriel whatever happens. He is certain—"

"Mrs. Gabriel has her flashlight turned on now!" Connie reported from the window. "She's examining something she has dug up!"

"It's not a tulip bulb either," added Rosemary.

"Let's go down there right now!" Vevi urged, again starting for the door.

"No, Vevi!" Miss Gordon checked her once more. "It would only frighten her away. We must wait for the police."

"They'll never come," complained Sunny. "It's been ages now."

Magic Ways

"Only a minute or two," corrected Miss Mohr. "Patience."

"The police will come," added the Brownie Scout leader.

She was right too. In less than ten minutes, the girls heard the high pitched, whining whistle of a siren.

"There they come!" cried Vevi. "I'm going down there now!"

Without even stopping to put on her cap or jacket she darted out the door. The other Brownies followed after her, in their excitement stumbling on the stairs.

Just as the group reached the street, the police car halted at the curb.

Mrs. Gabriel straightened up and then started hastily away. But the police did not let her escape.

Quickly they overtook her, grasping her firmly by the arm.

While one officer held Mrs. Gabriel, another questioned Miss Mohr and Miss Gordon as to the nature of their complaint.

"This woman has been destroying library property," declared Miss Mohr.

"We saw her digging up the Brownie Scout tulip bed," added Vevi. "I think she has some of our bulbs in her pocket now."

"Ridiculous!" snapped Mrs. Gabriel. "I suppose it does seem unusual for me to be found here digging up tulip bulbs. Nevertheless, I can explain."

"Please do," invited Miss Mohr.

"I bought a large order of tulips, especially valuable stock, from Mr. Mattox. Unfortunately, in driving home, I offered one of these children a ride."

"Me," interposed Vevi.

"She had a bag of worthless bulbs with her—"

"Not worthless," corrected Vevi. "They may have been culls but they were Golden Beauties. Those are the best and most valuable kind on the market now that Mr. Van Der Lann has won the blue ribbon!"

"If you'll keep quiet for a moment, I'll explain," said Mrs. Gabriel, glaring at Vevi. "The child either deliberately or possibly by mistake, exchanged a bag of my good bulbs for her trash. So tonight I thought to recover my stock."

The two police officers seemed half inclined to believe the woman's story.

"If it were only tulip bulbs you wanted, why

Magic Ways

didn't you come to Miss Mohr or me?" questioned the Brownie Scout leader.

"I realize I should have asked permission to dig up the bed," replied Mrs. Gabriel glibly. "I hesitated to do so because I didn't want to cause trouble."

"You set great store by those tulip bulbs," remarked Miss Mohr.

As she spoke, she glanced about the ground. The bulbs had been scattered everywhere. In her haste to dig them up. Mrs. Gabriel had broken many and chopped others in two with her sharp tool.

"If you valued your tulips so much, why did you dump all the other bags of bulbs along the roadside?" Vevi demanded.

Mrs. Gabriel ignored the pointed question, so the little girl asked it again.

"I don't know what you're talking about," the woman finally replied. "If you found any bulbs along the road, they must have belonged to someone else."

The police officers had been listening to the talk. Now one of the men had a question of his own.

"Lady," he said, "are you sure it was tulip bulbs you were after?"

181

"Of course! What else?"

"Sorry," said the policeman, "but I'm afraid we'll have to take you to the station for a complete search."

"The idea!" Mrs. Gabriel snapped. "You may look in my purse now if you like. You'll find nothing."

She offered her pocketbook, which the policeman thoroughly examined. Inside were toilet articles, a billfold containing nearly two hundred dollars, a handkerchief and a set of car keys.

"I saw her put something in her outside coat pocket while she was digging," Connie reported.

One of the officers reached into Mrs. Gabriel's pocket. He brought out nothing but an old theater program.

In the other coat pocket was an old handkerchief. One corner had been tied into a knot to hold several small objects.

"What's this?" commented the policeman, untying the handkerchief.

The cloth contained four dark-colored pellets.

"Our fertilizer!" exclaimed Vevi. "Well, what do you know! She was after our fertilizer, not the tulip bulbs!"

Magic Ways

Carefully the policeman examined the pellets. He rolled them between his fingers.

"You see, they are nothing!" said Mrs. Gabriel. "Now will you let me go? I've had quite enough of Rosedale and Brownie Scouts. I assure you I'll leave town promptly and not come back."

Before the officers could decide what to do, a car pulled up at the curb.

"There's Peter!" exclaimed Miss Mohr in relief.

The nurseryman leaped out of his car and came over to the flower bed. Miss Mohr told him what had happened before his arrival. The policeman showed him the pellets taken from Mrs. Gabriel.

"Just as I thought!" Mr. Van Der Lann exclaimed "These pellets are uncut commercial diamonds. They were smuggled to this country from Holland in a shipment of imported tulip bulbs."

"Then we planted diamonds, thinking it was fertilizer!" gasped Jane.

Mr. Van Der Lann's disclosure amazed everyone except Miss Mohr. She was not surprised because the nurseryman earlier had told her of his suspicion that Mrs. Gabriel was not an honest person.

Now that Mr. Van Der Lann had revealed that the pellets were uncut diamonds, the Brownie

Scouts became highly excited. Vevi was especially so, for she knew that Mrs. Gabriel had not had time to dig up all of the stones.

"Almost every tulip bulb has a pellet with it," she revealed. "Why, this old flower bed is full of diamonds!"

"I'm going to dig them up!" cried Jane, reaching for Mrs. Gabriel's trowel.

The police, however, would not permit any of the children or the adults to touch the flower bed. They said they would assign men to sift the earth and make certain that every uncut stone was recovered.

Mrs. Gabriel realized by this time that it was useless to deny her guilt.

"All right, I did smuggle the diamonds in with a shipment of bulbs," she acknowledged. "I wasn't alone in the deal though. If you arrest me, how about the Mattox couple?"

"We'll take care of them, never fear," the policeman assured her.

Mrs. Gabriel was taken away to the police station and other men came to sift the flower bed soil. All the Brownies, Mr. Van Der Lann, the librarian and

Magic Ways

Miss Gordon stood by, watching the work. Soon a fairly large crowd gathered.

"So Mr. and Mrs. Mattox are mixed up in this smuggling affair," remarked a businessman who paused to observe. "Well, that will finish the flower show."

"How do you mean?" inquired Miss Gordon.

"The Mattox couple contributed heavily for the affair. If they are arrested, they will not pay their assessment. Mr. Piff may as well call it quits."

As the digging went on, police talked at length with Mr. Van Der Lann. He was asked to relate everything he knew about Mrs. Gabriel and her smuggling activities.

"I met the woman for the first time a few weeks ago," the nurseryman revealed. "She came to Windmill Farm and proposed that I go in with her on her crooked scheme. At the time I needed money badly, but I refused."

"Uncle Peter ordered her to stay away from our place," added Hanny, who stood beside the nurseryman, watching the digging work.

"That is true," agreed Mr. Van Der Lann. "When she learned she could not do business with me, she took up with Mr. and Mrs. Mattox. As to their part in the affair, I can only guess. My suspicion is that they cooperated with Mrs. Gabriel fully in importing bulbs which they knew were only a cover for a shipment of priceless commercial stones."

"You and Mr. Mattox have never been good friends," commented one of the policemen.

"That is so," agreed the nurseryman. "Always Mr. and Mrs. Mattox have considered me as a business rival. They sought to add my farm to their own. Of late they have been especially eager to get me out of the community, fearing no doubt that I would expose their association with Mrs. Gabriel."

"They will make you no more trouble," the policeman promised. "The sheriff has been asked to arrest the couple for questioning. Very shortly they will be taken to jail."

The digging work went on. Within an hour every diamond had been recovered.

However, the flower bed was completely ruined. Dirt had been scattered everywhere and only a few of the tulip bulbs were worth saving.

"Vevi, whatever possessed you girls to plant tulip bulbs at this time of year?" Miss Gordon questioned.

Magic Ways

"They should be planted in the fall, you know, for spring blooms."

"We didn't want spring flowers though," Vevi explained. "We wanted tulips right now."

"While the flower show is on," declared Jane.

Miss Gordon regretfully told the Brownies that seeds or plants would have to be used if the troop were to have a flower bed that year. Even if they went to work at once, the bed would not be in bloom for several weeks.

The information made all the Brownies unhappy, especially Vevi.

"I did so want tulips," she said. "They are the most beautiful flower in the world. Now I've even lost my Golden Beauty culls."

"Don't worry about that," said Mr. Van Der Lann "Next Spring I will give you some choice stock."

Vevi thanked the nurseryman, but continued to look unhappy. "I wanted a tulip bed so badly," she murmured.

"So did I," said Jane. "It was fun catching Mrs. Gabriel and saving the diamonds, but I'd rather have had a beautiful bed of flowers."

"Do all the Brownies feel the same way about

tulips?" inquired Mr. Van Der Lann. "Would they rather have them than any other flower?"

"Oh, yes!" cried Vevi. "But it is impossible. We will have to wait until next year."

"And that is a million years away," sighed Sunny.

"Perhaps not," said Mr. Van Der Lann. He smiled in a most mysterious sort of way.

"What do you mean?" questioned Vevi alertly.

"Just you wait!" he advised. "Not a year either."

Now the Brownie Scouts sensed immediately that their friend had something special in mind. They teased him to tell what it was.

Mr. Van Der Lann only smiled and shook his head.

"I can guess!" laughed Hanny.

"Tell us," pleaded the other Brownies.

Hanny grinned and would not answer. "It's a secret," she chuckled. "Nurserymen sometimes have magic ways. Just you wait!"

Chapter 19

AN ANNOUNCEMENT

VEVI awoke late the next morning, feeling tired in every bone and muscle. Pulling herself slowly up in bed, she peered out the window. It was raining hard.

"Oh, dear," she thought. "I did so hope for a nice day."

Vevi dressed and went downstairs for a belated breakfast.

"Mother," she said, seating herself at the table by the kitchen window. "Is it really true that Mrs. Gabriel was caught digging up the Brownie Scout flower bed last night? Or did I dream it?"

Mrs. McGuire handed her the morning paper.

"It was true, Vevi. See, the story of what happened is on the front page. The Brownies are mentioned too."

Vevi read every word of the story for herself. The item told of Mrs. Gabriel's arrest and confinement in jail. Related also, was the part the Brownies had played in the capture.

"Oh, by the way," Mrs. McGuire said after the little girl had finished her breakfast. "Miss Mohr telephoned a few minutes ago. All the Brownies are to meet at the library directly after lunch. She said something about an extra special surprise."

"But the Brownies had a meeting last night, Mother. Why are we meeting again so soon?"

"She didn't say, dear."

"Maybe it is about our flower bed," Vevi speculated. "I think that must be it."

The little girl helped her mother with the housework. She dusted the furniture and wiped dishes. Time seemed to pass very slowly. All the while, she kept speculating upon why Miss Mohr would call a special meeting of the Brownie troop.

As soon as luncheon was over, Vevi changed into her Brownie uniform. Carrying her red umbrella, she splashed along the sloppy streets toward the library. It was not raining much now, but the gutters ran deep with muddy water.

Vevi had not gone many blocks when she had to wait at an intersection for a traffic light.

As she stood there, a taxi came up very fast. The light changed and the cab halted with a screech of

An Announcement

brakes. It stopped so suddenly beside Vevi, that she felt her legs being splashed with dirty water.

She jumped back, very much annoyed at the driver.

"Sorry," apologized the cab man, leaning out of the taxi window. "I shouldn't have tried to make the light, but my customer is in a big rush to catch a train."

Vevi glanced into the back of the cab and was surprised to see that the passenger was Mr. Piff.

"Why, are you leaving Rosedale?" she asked.

"Am I?" he replied. "The flower show is washed up—finished. This rain was the last straw. I'm getting out of this hick town for good."

"Rosedale is nice," Vevi answered. "It's not a hick town—"

She had no chance to say more. Just then the light changed to green again. The cab sped on, disappearing down the street.

Crossing the street, Vevi went on to the library. She glanced quickly toward the flower bed.

To her disappointment, it appeared exactly as it had the previous night. Dirt was scattered everywhere on the grass and so were the broken tulip bulbs.

"I guess Peter Van Der Lann was joking about magic," she thought. "Nothing is changed."

All of the Brownies except Hanny had arrived at the library ahead of Vevi. As soon as she came into the story room, Miss Gordon and Miss Mohr signaled for silence.

"Girls," the librarian announced, "we have all been invited to Peter's—I mean to Mr. Van Der Lann's home for a little outing. This rain has rather spoiled our plans, but I'm sure we'll have a fine time in any event."

"Will we have to walk?" Rosemary asked, rather dismayed. "I didn't bring my umbrella or a raincoat."

Miss Mohr assured the girls that the nurseryman would come for them in his truck. He was expected at any moment.

"He's here now," reported Connie a moment later. She had been watching from the window. "He's driving up in front."

"Come girls," urged Miss Gordon. "We mustn't keep him waiting."

The Brownies put on their coats and went outside.

"Why, it's stopped raining!" cried Jane, holding

An Announcement

up her hand to see if she could catch any drops. "The sun is trying to peek through a cloud."

"We'll have a fine day yet!" exclaimed Sunny. "Hurrah for Windmill Farm!"

Mr. Van Der Lann helped the children into the truck. Miss Mohr and the Brownie leader rode up front.

During the ride to the farm, the nurseryman was in very high spirits. He declared that everything had gone extremely well for him and for Hanny.

"Now that I have won first prize for the Golden Beauty tulip, nearly everyone wants to buy my stock of bulbs," he said. "I have arranged to sell them all to one eastern dealer at a very high price."

"I will get to stay in America," added Hanny happily.

Mr. Van Der Lann had arranged a pleasant afternoon for the Brownies at Windmill Farm. He told the girls they might pick all the tulips they liked, ride in the dog cart and even in the boat.

"Not the boat," laughed Vevi. "It leaks."

"Oh, I repaired it yesterday," the nurseryman assured her. "Mr. and Mrs. Mattox will not annoy you either, should you drift past their place. The sheriff took them to jail today for questioning."

"Then it has been established that they aided Mrs. Gabriel?" questioned Miss Gordon.

"Yes, they worked with her in smuggling gems into this country from Holland. I long suspected it, but could prove nothing and so remained quiet."

"I guess the Brownies were pretty smart to catch Mrs. Gabriel digging up the tulips!" Vevi chuckled.

At Windmill Farm, the Brownies found Hanny and the housekeeper busy in the spic and span kitchen. The room was fragrant with the smell of baking. Little cakes had been taken from the oven and now were being beautifully frosted.

"Why, we must be having a party!" laughed Connie.

Now the Brownies could not imagine why everyone seemed so happy at Windmill Farm. Nor could they understand the reason Mr. Van Der Lann had gone to so much trouble just for them.

"I think someone is keeping a secret from us," guessed Connie. "Isn't that right?"

"It could be," admitted Miss Mohr.

"Tell us!" pleaded Rosemary.

"Later—"

"Right now!" teased the Brownies.

An Announcement

"Shall we tell them?" Miss Mohr asked, turning to Hanny's uncle.

"Why keep them in suspense?" he replied. "Let the news be known."

"I want to pass the little cakes!" cried Hanny in excitement.

She made everyone sit in the living room. Then she passed the refreshments, giving every Brownie one of the delicately frosted cakes.

Now the girls were not very hungry, having finished their lunches only a short while before. Being polite, however, they did not mention this.

Vevi was the first to break open her little cake.

"Why, there's a piece of paper in mine!" she exclaimed.

"Read it," urged Hanny. "I already know the good news."

Vevi spread out the strip of paper. Two names had been printed on it. She read them aloud.

"Peter Van Der Lann and Miss Mohr!" she exclaimed, not understanding why the names had been baked into the cake.

"Peter and I are to be married in a few days," the librarian announced. "We decided to have the wedding so soon because Peter must go to New York with his tulip bulbs. We'll call it our honeymoon."

Now the Brownies were delighted to hear that Miss Mohr was to wed. They were especially glad that Hanny would have someone as nice as the librarian to look after her.

"If you are to be married right away, I don't suppose there will be a big wedding," Vevi remarked.

"Oh, we couldn't omit that," smiled the librarian. "We plan a wonderful church wedding. Hanny is to be the ring bearer. I want all the Brownies to be there."

"As bridesmaids?" Vevi asked quickly.

Miss Mohr explained that Miss Gordon and some of her older friends would act as maids. She promised though that the Brownies would have a special pew in the church.

After refreshments had been enjoyed, the Brownies went outside to play. Never had Windmill Farm looked so beautiful. The rain had made the grass fresh and green. Tulips were bent over and heavy with water, but the bright sun was reviving them.

"I want to ride in the boat!" declared Connie quickly.

An Announcement

"I'm going to pick tulips." announced Rosemary. "A bouquet of nothing but bright pink ones."

"I want to pick flowers too," declared Jane. "My bouquet will be purple."

Sunny announced that she intended to watch the windmill for awhile and then ride with Connie in the boat.

"What will you do, Vevi?" asked Hanny.

Vevi had been thinking over her choice very carefully.

"I will ride in the dog cart," she announced. "I want that old Bruno to know who is boss!"

While the others went toward the tulip fields, Hanny and Vevi ran to the barn to find the dog. They hitched him to the cart. Vevi climbed in and picked up the reins.

"Now start him easy," Hanny instructed. "If he tries to run away again, I will punish him."

The big dog however, seemed to know that with Hanny there, he could not play tricks. When Vevi said "Giddap!" he moved off at a very slow walk.

After a minute or two, the little girl wished that he would go faster. Bruno though, did not feel like trotting or running. He ambled lazily toward the cheese house and then on past the little house where

Mr. Van Der Lann had stored his Golden Beauty tulip bulbs.

Vevi noticed that the door no longer was locked.

"I guess your uncle has moved his bulbs somewhere else," she remarked to Hanny who was walking along beside the cart.

"What?" inquired Hanny, not understanding.

Vevi repeated what she had said, and pointed to the open door.

Hanny stopped short, staring at it.

"That door shouldn't be open!" she cried. "I'm sure Uncle Peter hasn't moved the bulbs. We have always kept them there."

Hanny ran over to the little house. Vevi dropped the reins and scrambled out of the dog cart. Thus released, Bruno trotted off toward the canal. Neither of the girls noticed.

Hanny had reached the open door. She pushed it back so she could look at the padlock.

"It has been broken!" she exclaimed. "Oh, Vevi!"

Hanny darted into the room where the precious Golden Beauty tulip bulbs had been stored. Vevi kept close behind.

It was dark inside though, and she could see nothing.

An Announcement

Hanny groped for the light switch and finally found it. As she switched it on, the room was fully illuminated.

Both girls looked quickly at the wall shelves. All of the tulip bulbs were gone!

"Someone has taken them!" gasped Hanny. "A wicked thief has broken in here and stolen Uncle Peter's Golden Beauty stock!"

Chapter 20

SURPRISE!

THOROUGHLY alarmed, Vevi and Hanny ran as fast as they could to the house to relate what had happened.

"Uncle Peter! Uncle Peter!" Hanny shouted, bursting into the house. "Come quick!"

"Why, what is wrong?" he inquired. Startled, he rose quickly to his feet, fearing that one of the Brownies had been hurt.

"Our tulip bulbs!" Hanny cried. "Did you move them from the little house?"

"No, Hanny, I did not."

"Then they have been stolen!" Hanny was so excited that she began to speak in Dutch, telling her uncle of the discovery she and Vevi had made.

Mr. Van Der Lann ran to the storehouse to see for himself.

"Gone!" he groaned as he too beheld the empty shelves.

"Maybe it was Mr. Evans who took the bulbs,"

Surprise!

guessed Vevi, remembering that she had seen the man examining the padlock a few days earlier.

"No! No! It could not have been he," insisted the nurseryman. "Mr. Evans is a federal agent. He was sent here to try to catch the smugglers. I talked to him only last night and he now has left Rosedale."

"Mr. Piff is going away too," remarked Vevi.

"Mr. Piff!" exclaimed the nurseryman. "When did you last see him?"

"Only a minute or two before we came out here in your truck. He was in a taxi cab."

"What made you think he was leaving Rosedale, Vevi?"

"He said so. He said the show had failed, and he was going away. The taxi was taking him to a train."

"The show was a failure all right," declared Mr. Van Der Lann. "But Mr. Piff has no call to go away without making a full accounting to the townspeople who contributed to his flower fund. He has run up many debts. Besides, I suspect he may be the one who took my bulbs!"

"Not Mr. Piff?" echoed Miss Gordon. "How could he do such a thing?"

"He has been here several times during the last few days," the nurseryman revealed. "When he saw that his show would fail, he sought a means of making quick money. He wanted to sell my bulbs for me, but I turned him down."

"Did he know where you kept them, Peter?" asked Miss Mohr.

"Yes, and he was here this morning while I was at the library. The housekeeper told me so."

"Can't we stop him from leaving Rosedale?" Miss Gordon asked. She look at her wristwatch, and added:

"His train may have gone by this time. There is a chance, though, that we can intercept him."

"I will try," said Mr. Van Der Lann grimly.

He ran to get his truck. By this time, Connie and Sunny had run up from the canal. Jane and Rosemary, their arms laden with tulips, raced in from the fields to see what was happening.

"Everyone into the truck!" ordered Mr. Van Der Lann.

The Brownies scrambled in, fairly tumbling over one another in their haste.

"Those bulbs represent my entire fortune," Mr. Van Der Lann declared, starting off very fast. "I must get them back."

Surprise!

Rosedale had only one union station. The nurseryman drove directly there. Passengers could be seen waiting on the platform. Luggage had been piled up on a dolly-truck ready to be hauled to the train when it came in.

Even as the Brownies leaped from Mr. Van Der Lann's truck, they heard the whistle of the approaching engine.

"Hurry! Hurry!" urged Vevi. "It's coming now."

Passengers were gathering up their hand luggage. The children did not see Mr. Piff anywhere.

"He must have taken an earlier train," declared Miss Gordon anxiously. "I'm afraid we have missed him."

"I'll look in the depot," offered Vevi.

"You don't need to!" cried Connie excitedly. "There he comes now!"

Mr. Piff had left the building and was walking directly toward the group.

Suddenly he saw the Brownies with Mr. Van Der Lann, and stopped short. He turned as if to move in the opposite direction.

"Wait!" called the nurseryman.

Mr. Piff reluctantly obeyed the command.

The Brownie Scouts at Windmill Farm

"Well?" he demanded. "What do you want?"

The train now was very close. Mr. Van Der Lann knew he would have to talk fast.

"You cannot leave Rosedale without making an accounting of the flower show funds!" he told the promoter. "Debts are not paid and you have all the money."

"Try to stop me," said Mr. Piff unpleasantly. "I'm fed up with this town. I'm leaving."

"Oh, no, you are not," corrected the nurseryman. He spoke quietly but with firmness.

By this time the train had pulled into the station. Most of the passengers already had boarded their cars.

"Get out of my way!" Mr. Piff said furiously.

He tried to push past the nurseryman. Mr. Van Der Lann grasped him by the arm, making the promoter drop one of the bags he carried.

Vevi snatched it up. Before anyone could stop her, she had opened it.

Inside were two sacks of tulip bulbs. Vevi knew at once that they were the Golden Beauties.

"So!" exclaimed Mr. Van Der Lann. "I thought as much."

"Now see here," said Mr. Piff, still trying to pull

Surprise!

away. "I can explain. It's true I intended to sell the bulbs to a dealer I know. But you would have received the full amount, minus a small commission. I can get you a much better price than you can arrange for yourself."

Mr. Van Der Lann paid no attention. He went through the promoter's luggage, taking all the bulbs that were his.

Then he made Mr. Piff turn over all the money he had collected for his flower show from Rosedale townspeople.

"Now get on that train and never come back here!" the nurseryman said, shoving him toward his car.

"You're not having me arrested?" Mr. Piff muttered.

"Get on your train," the nurseryman ordered again. "And let this be a lesson to you."

Mr. Piff grabbed up his luggage, including the empty handbag, and ran for the train. He swung aboard. The cars began to move, slowly at first and then faster and faster.

"Goodbye, Mr. Piff!" laughed Sunny.

Mr. Van Der Lann pocketed the money he had taken from the promoter. He told Miss Mohr and

The Brownie Scouts at Windmill Farm

the Brownie Scout leader that he doubted it would be enough to pay all of the flower show debts.

"It will cover most of the expense though," he assured the women. "I will turn all of this money over to Mrs. Langley or the Chamber of Commerce president."

Now the Brownies were happy indeed that the nurseryman had recovered the Golden Beauty tulip bulbs. Mr. Van Der Lann assured them that he would ship the bulbs east that very day so that there would be no risk of having them stolen again.

For the troop members, the day had been a thrilling one. During the next week they had many wonderful times too, going often to Windmill Farm.

Miss Mohr especially, was kept very busy, planning her approaching wedding. Often the Brownies went with her to the stores to help her buy finery. Time was very short, and it seemed there were a million things to do.

Then finally, the important day was at hand.

All the Brownies, dressed in fresh Scout uniforms, arrived early at the church. An usher escorted them to their seats, a special roped-off pew at the front.

"I hope everything goes off well," Vevi whispered

Surprise!

nervously to Connie. "Wouldn't it be awful if Hanny should drop the ring?"

"Sh!" Connie warned severely. "The ceremony is starting."

An expectant hush had fallen upon the church throng. The organist began to play a solemn wedding march.

"Here they come!" whispered Rosemary, twisting around to see. "Oh, how lovely!"

Hanny led the stately procession down the carpeted aisle. She was dressed in white, and carried a basket of flower petals which she dropped one by one ahead of the bride.

Miss Mohr wore a white satin gown with long train and a veil. Her flowers were Golden Beauty tulips. She had never been more lovely.

"Doesn't Miss Gordon look nice too?" murmured Connie.

The Brownie Scout leader was dressed in pink, with a large picture hat. She and the other bridesmaids carried bouquets of tulips also.

At the proper moment in the ceremony, the ring was produced. Then the minister spoke the words which made Miss Mohr and Mr. Van Der Lann man and wife.

"There! It's over!" Vevi whispered. "Now we can throw our rice!"

As soon as the procession had passed out of the church, the Brownie Scouts hastened to the exit.

They were in time to see the bridal party getting into cars.

"Now for the rice!" chuckled Vevi.

Each Brownie Scout had brought a small bag filled with rice grains. Laughing and shouting, they hurled it at the bridal couple.

Miss Mohr leaned out of the car to speak to the girls.

"Peter and I will soon return from our honeymoon," she said. "When we do, we want you all to come often to visit us at Windmill Farm."

"We will," promised Connie, speaking for all the Brownies.

"One more thing," said Miss Mohr. "I have a special request."

"What is it, Miss Mohr—I mean Mrs. Van Der Lann?" inquired Vevi politely.

"I want all the Brownies to walk past the library when they leave the church."

Surprise!

Now Vevi thought this a most strange request indeed.

"Past the library?" she repeated, thinking that possibly the librarian had made a slip of tongue.

"Yes, dear, it's a surprise. From Peter."

Vevi and the other Brownies were more mystified than ever. Before they could ask a single question, the cars began to move away.

Mr. Van Der Lann opened a paper sack. He began to toss cellophane-wrapped candies to the children.

"*Suikers,*" he explained with a smile. "Sugar plums. It's an old Dutch custom to throw them at every wedding."

The Brownies caught most of the sugar plums. Jane, who was agile, picked up four, and Vevi captured three. The other girls had at least one or two apiece.

The bridal cars rounded a corner and were gone. For just a minute, the Brownie Scouts felt lonesome.

"What shall we do now?" asked Sunny. "Go home?"

"We must walk past the library," Connie said,

recalling Miss Mohr's final instructions. "I wonder why she asked us to do it?"

"It is out of my way to go that direction," declared Rosemary. "Do you think it would matter if I walk past some other time?"

"No, we must all go now—together," Vevi insisted. "Miss Mohr said it was important."

"That's right," agreed Connie. "She spoke of a surprise. One from Peter."

The girls started off, walking in pairs. Vevi and Connie were ahead, followed by the others.

"What surprise could Peter have left for us?" Vevi speculated.

"A package of books perhaps," Rosemary guessed.

"He may have given the troop a piece of his fine Delft ware," Sunny declared. "I would like that for a gift."

Thinking of various possibilities, the girls began to walk faster. Soon they came within view of the library.

"How will we know about the surprise?" Jane asked in perplexity. "Are we supposed to go into the building and ask one of the librarians?"

"Well, if we aren't dopes!" suddenly cried Vevi. She stopped short and began to laugh.

Surprise!

"What's wrong with you?" demanded Jane.

"The surprise!" cried Vevi. "One can see it a mile away! It's a wonderful one too!"

The other Brownies were bewildered by the little girl's words. But only for a moment.

"Oh, I see it too!" exclaimed Connie.

She and Vevi both began to run toward the library.

Then Jane, Rosemary and Sunny joined the race.

The surprise, everyone now knew, was a beautiful flower bed!

As the girls aproached closer, they could see it plainly.

The circular bed which Miss Mohr had given to the Brownie Scouts for their very own, now was a mass of blooms.

Yellow and gold and brown tulips blazed in the sunlight. The Brownies never had seen a more gorgeous sight.

"Oh, it's wonderful!" cried Vevi, dancing about the bed. "Just what I wanted!"

"It's our very own too!" added Sunny.

"Look at the center of the bed," directed Connie.

Mr. Van Der Lann had so arranged the tulips that they resembled the clover-shaped Scout emblem.

The letters "G. S." were spelled out in bright yellow tulips.

"That stands for Girl Scouts," commented Jane. "I do wish Mr. Van Der Lann had made a 'B' to stand for Brownie."

"All Brownie Scouts fly up to become Girl Scouts when they're old enough," declared Connie. "I like our flower bed just as he made it."

"So do I," agreed Rosemary. "I think this is the nicest surprise our troop ever had."

"The very best," echoed Sunny.

"How do you suppose Mr. Van Der Lann made the tulips grow so fast?" speculated Jane. "Why, it's almost miraculous!"

"He couldn't have planted bulbs, that's certain," replied Connie. "I know! He must have brought potted plants from Windmill Farm!"

"However he did it, I guess it proves the Brownie Story," asserted Vevi.

The other girls asked her what she meant.

Vevi grinned happily and bent down to sniff the fragrance of a big yellow tulip. Then with twinkling eyes, she replied:

"Don't you see? It's magic, pure magic!"

Surprise!

"It does seem almost like it," admitted Connie.

"This wonderful surprise proves that elves are still at work," Vevi said with a laugh. "They live in Rosedale and everywhere in the world. And best of all, they serve the Brownies!"

THE END